HOPE
IS NOT
A PLAN

BUILDING ONE OF AMERICA'S
FASTEST GROWING COMPANIES

HOPE
IS NOT
A PLAN

DOUG CALLAHAN

Advantage.

Published by Advantage, Charleston, South Carolina.
Member of Advantage Media Group, Inc.

ADVANTAGE is a registered trademark, and the Advantage colophon is a trademark of Advantage Media Group, Inc.

Printed in the United States of America.

10 9 8 7 6 5 4 3 2 1

ISBN: 978-1-64225-103-6
LCCN: 2019914028

Cover and layout design by Wesley Strickland.

Cover photo: Michael Guimond.

This publication is designed to provide accurate and authoritative information in regard to the subject matter covered. It is sold with the understanding that the publisher is not engaged in rendering legal, accounting, or other professional services. If legal advice or other expert assistance is required, the services of a competent professional person should be sought.

Advantage Media Group is proud to be a part of the Tree Neutral® program. Tree Neutral offsets the number of trees consumed in the production and printing of this book by taking proactive steps such as planting trees in direct proportion to the number of trees used to print books. To learn more about Tree Neutral, please visit **www.treeneutral.com**.

Advantage Media Group is a publisher of business, self-improvement, and professional development books and online learning. We help entrepreneurs, business leaders, and professionals share their Stories, Passion, and Knowledge to help others Learn & Grow. Do you have a manuscript or book idea that you would like us to consider for publishing? Please visit **advantagefamily.com** or call **1.866.775.1696**.

Thank you to my mother, who taught me the value of an education and work ethic. She taught me I can achieve anything I want in life if I work hard for it.

CONTENTS

INTRODUCTION

I love being a business owner. When I leave my house in the morning, I don't feel as if I'm going to work; I feel as if I'm charging out the door to make things happen in an industry I love. And I think I'm pretty good at it. Back in 2012, I bought my first company, MMI Engineered Solutions, and we've since *quadrupled* our growth. Today my business employs more than two hundred people in two countries and was recently recognized by *Inc.* magazine as one of America's fastest-growing companies, while I was recently named a 2018 Ernst & Young Entrepreneur of the Year. We have exceptional clients, and we're recognized as best in class across all of our industry's benchmarks. In 2018 we did $40 million in annual sales; we have more than $60 million booked for 2019—a 50 percent jump. By the time you read this book, I hope to have dwarfed all those numbers. In short, MMI is firing on all cylinders.

I feel as if I was born to run this business. I can't imagine doing anything else.

I didn't always feel this way. I didn't always even want to be a business owner. I spent many years happily working for others. I was a designer and engineer in an injection-molded plastics company serving the auto industry. And honestly, I loved my job. I developed new products and ideas. I traveled all around the world. I met fascinating people. I managed teams. I developed new business. I made a mark in an industry I loved. I was happy; I really was.

There finally came a day, though, when I realized my growth had reached its upper limits within the bounds of salaried employment. I was presented with an opportunity to take everything I'd learned in nineteen years of working for a private company and apply that same recipe to a business *I* owned. I pulled the trigger, and it was the best decision I ever made.

Since that time I've achieved levels of satisfaction that simply would not have been possible as someone's employee, and I have completely redefined what success means to me. Owning a business has been a quantum leap for me, one whose benefits I couldn't have entirely foreseen from my old position as an employee. You won't find a bigger fan of business ownership on this planet than me.

So does that mean owning a business is right for everyone? Absolutely not. A great surgeon may not need or want to own the hospital he works in. Many of the best business leaders of our era have been salaried CEOs and presidents who did not own their companies. I personally speak from the standpoint of a passionate owner, but my intention in these pages is to show you the mind-set, decision-making, and personal qualities it takes to be a thriving business *leader*— whether you own your business or not. So when I use the term "ownership," understand that I mean it in the larger sense of *taking ultimate responsibility*. If you're in a position to lead a business in any capacity whatsoever—or you're just interested in *learning* about business leadership—this book will give you my recipe for getting it right.

This book is a distillation of everything I've learned in my career, not just in my years as a business owner, but in all those years leading up to being a business owner, when I was figuring all this stuff out and making a lot of valuable mistakes. I believe if you take its messages to heart, you will cut out years of costly trial and error, and you will exponentially multiply your long-term odds of success in business—no matter what level of leadership you're at.

MY STORY

First, a bit about me, so you'll know whose advice you're about to swallow—or ignore, as the case may be. Like many who've gone on to success, I had a rather inauspicious start in life. I'm the youngest of five kids, and life threw me its first big curveball when I was eighteen months old: my father died. My mom, who had never worked a day in her life, suddenly found herself alone with a house full of screaming kids and zero job skills. Five kids, no income, no résumé. With a different mom at the helm, we probably would have ended up in foster care, all of us. But my mother went out and found a job working for General Motors—a turning point for all of us—and then worked several other jobs to help support us. She never gave up, never complained (well, *almost* never).

We were an automotive family, and I took a liking to cars and designing things when I was quite young. I hit on my career path the day I walked into high school at the start of ninth grade and sat down in my drafting class. I knew in that moment I wanted to go into engineering and be involved in the design and development of cars.

There is no question as to where I acquired my drive to work hard and my passion to build a successful business. It all came from watching my mother struggling and clawing her way ahead, trying to make life better for us. I entered the educational and working world with a huge leg up: the work ethic I had inherited from my mom.

I went to engineering school right out of high school and spent four years working for General Motors in the design department while I was going through college. My whole family, in fact, was attached at some point in our lives to General Motors and the auto industry in Detroit. You might say making cars is in our blood. We all went to college, too, and did pretty well for ourselves. Thanks, Mom.

In '93 I graduated from engineering school, and GM was not hiring engineers at the time. I wanted to get out of the design area and become an engineer, so I took a job working for an automotive supplier. It was a relatively small, family-owned company—a $20 million company that made injection-molded plastic components for the auto industry. Over the ensuing years, I took on progressively more responsibility and ended up staying with that employer for nineteen years. During that time, I helped build a ragtag $20 million-a-year company into a $300 million success story. We were squarely in the middle of a major movement, at the time, to get rid of rubber and metal in automobiles and convert many parts to plastic. I was heavily involved in that movement.

I was loyal to the company, but my ambitions ran high. While working there full time, I went to graduate school four nights a week and got my MBA in global business operations. I later went to law school on the same type of schedule and got my doctorate in patent law. I viewed these educational achievements as adding tools to my tool belt so that I could take on more responsibility in the company. While I was doing all that, I also helped open new operations in Mexico, Tennessee, and Japan while remaining deeply involved in new product and new business development. I acquired a lot of customer interface experience as well and did quite a bit of internal team-building. With all the schooling, travel, eighteen-hour workdays, and overlapping job responsibilities I'd taken on, I felt as if

I'd gained about fifty years of experience in my less than two decades at the company. I was primed for leadership.

Then one day a fateful change occurred. The family ownership group decided to replace the company president. I'll tell you more of this story in the next chapter, but the short version is: they didn't hire me. I stayed on for three more years, watching the man they *did* hire drive a fine company into the ground while I champed at the bit to jump in and right the ship. I realized my career growth had gone as far as it could go within the bounds of this company.

At this point, destiny intervened. I learned about a small injection-molding company that was looking for new leadership. Long story short, I acquired the company, and the rest is the history we are happily writing every day. Our growth has been astonishing, and the awards keep piling up. (Literally, as I write these words, we just received the prestigious Strategically Focused Award from the state of Michigan.)

It hasn't been easy to get to where we are today. In fact, it's been one crazy hurdle after another. But one thing I've learned as an owner is that the hurdles are the good stuff. The hurdles are what force you to stretch and grow. And in the end, the hurdles are the source of your personal fulfillment too. Knowing that you encountered huge obstacles and turned them around by hiring the right people and executing the right strategies provides the kind of satisfaction one can only achieve as the ultimate leader of a business.

TWO IMPORTANT MENTAL STEPS

Before we start to dig into what outstanding business ownership/leadership is all about, there are two things I'd like you to think about, right out of the starting gate—two important mental steps you can take at the outset if you are serious about going into business for yourself. Getting right in these two areas will make all the difference in the world as you launch into this exciting new phase of your career. These ideas should be percolating in the back of your mind as you read the rest of the book.

1. **Be prepared to give it everything.** Know from the start that owning a business is not for the fainthearted, the lazy, or the hopers versus doers. Being a business owner is not just your *job*; it's your *life*, and you need to approach it that way from day one. If you think you're going to just put in your forty hours a week and sit back and reap the profits, ownership may not be the right move for you.

    Your business needs to be your *everything*, especially in the early years. You need to live and breathe it, 24–7. Think about it day and night. Give all your energy to it, nonstop, without expecting anything in return. It's all give, no take, at least in the early days.

    That means sacrifice. It means other things must go, or at least be placed on the back burner. Time-consuming hobbies? Not anymore—your *business* is your new hobby. Relationships? Don't start any new ones, not right now. If you're already in a relationship, your significant other and/or family members must be fully on board with your decision to give this business your all. Political or social causes? Not now—your *business* is your cause. Later, when the business is successful, you can use it as a vehicle for giving back to your community. But right now, it's all about pouring everything you have into the business. Everything else is secondary.

    A big reason many people get this part wrong is that they choose the wrong business to get into. Motivated primarily by profit, they enter a business they don't personally care about. And that mind-set just doesn't work. In order to find the energy and commitment it's going to take to live and breathe your company 24–7, the business must be something *you are passionate about*. Money is not motivation enough.

Furthermore, the business must be one *you understand and to which you can add value*. Viewing a business primarily as a profit center is a formula for failure. Which brings us to the second point.

2. **Define what success means to you.** You must know what success actually *is*. That may sound obvious, but too few people think about what success really means beyond making a lot of money. Success must be considered on several different levels.

First, yes, there is **financial success**. Financial success, as a business, is easy to define, right? It includes factors such as gross margins, cost of goods sold, and so on. But ultimately, it's as simple as pointing to a number on your P&L statement and saying, "Hey, look, when I compare my bottom-line profitability to the industry standard, I'm doing well."

Unfortunately, that's as far as many people go with their thinking. You must go further.

There's also **industry success**. Just because you're financially successful (for now) does not mean you have achieved this higher milestone. Industry success is crucial if you want to have a lasting career in your field. Industry success means you have a profitable, *sustainable* business that has found its footing in your industry over the long term. That will never happen if you sacrifice long-term gains for short-term financial success.

Industry success is all about building a reputation. And to do that, you must understand your customers and what *they* judge you on—things like cost, service, dependability, quality, technology, and shipping costs. When defining industry success, I like to say, "I want customers who are important to me, but I'm important to them as well." When you have that kind of mutual relationship with a customer, that's when you can have long-term success. Because if the fit is wrong—if the value proposition you offer is not one that's coveted by your chosen customers—you're not going to be good partners together, and you're not going to last long in the business. Long-term industry success is hard to win. Know that.

Finally, there is what we can call **personal success**. What does success mean to you as a unique individual? When we see someone who owns a big house in a fancy zip code or drives a top-of-the-line car, we often say, "Wow, that person is very successful." But that person might be miserable and on the verge of a nervous breakdown. That's not success.

My own definition of success entails a lot of things. It starts with being able to organize a for-profit business through which I can build my own wealth, my own way, and secure a future for myself and my family. It also includes the ability to put a team together the way I want and to set my own metrics on how we track our progress. It means having the freedom to devise a business strategy and execute on that strategy on a daily basis. It means teaching and coaching a team of individuals, in different disciplines, and watching them grow as individuals and professionals. It means breaking industry barriers and innovating new technologies. And it means creating a value proposition that customers really want and having them come to me and say, "Thanks for doing that work for me. You guys do a great job."

So for me, the only way I can experience my definition of success is by owning my own business. But you must know *your own* definition of success—beyond the financial—before you make the leap. You might be the type of person who likes to focus on one skill or talent, such as playing the piano or designing buildings. Or you may be someone who is happiest when performing within an established structure someone else provides, or when working alone and away from other people.

But if your definition of success includes creating products and services you can pour your passion into, putting teams of great people together, facing new challenges every day, creating delighted customers, and making a mark in an industry you care about, then owning or leading a business might be the right choice for you.

If you're interested in becoming an exceptional business leader, or you're simply interested in learning about how a successful business works, read on …

CHAPTER 1

BECOMING A BUSINESS OWNER

Some people are born entrepreneurs. As kids they turn their lemonade stands into profitable enterprises and hire other kids to work for them. In college, they create laundry-washing services for their dormitories. They make their first million by the time they're twenty-two.

I wasn't one of those people. I *evolved* into a business owner. I simply loved the business I was in and wanted to play a larger and larger role in it. And I wasn't able to do that within the constraints of my old role.

If you keep a goldfish in a small tank, it will never grow larger than a few inches. But if you turn that goldfish loose in a pond, it will grow until it attains its fullest natural size. In my old job, I slowly began to sense that I was in a small tank that would never allow me to grow to my full size. And then a series of events happened that prompted me to jump out of that tank and into a bigger

I'd like to share that story with you, because it was through that story that I figured out, once and for all, what the heart of successful business is all about.

pond. I'd like to share that story with you, because it was through that story that I figured out, once and for all, what the heart of successful business is all about.

JUMPING OUT OF THE FISH TANK

In 2008, the auto industry was falling hard, and the molded plastics company I worked for was experiencing collateral damage. The majority of our business was in the auto industry. The company was family owned, as I've mentioned, and there were five family owner-operators in the business at the time. They took a look at the challenges in front of them and said, "Hey, we're either going to sell the company or turn it over to a new management team that has more energy than we do and get it ready for the next generation of family members." At that time, the next generation was still only six or eight years old, so the owners were looking for their new interim management team to carry and grow the business for a good many years.

I thought, in all modesty, that Douglas Callahan would make an excellent candidate to serve as the new president. Not only did I know virtually every aspect of the business inside out and sideways—product design, engineering, customer relations, sales, new business development; you name it—but I also had the right credentials to hang on a corner office wall: an MBA and a law doctorate. On top of that, I had a great relationship with the family owners. They trusted me and talked to me whenever they wanted to know what was really going on in the company. So I figured I'd be given top consideration.

I was wrong. The owners chose to pass me over. Why? Because they liked the stability and know-how I provided in my existing role. I was in charge of developing products and customer relationships, as well as innovating product. They didn't want to lose me in that role, and so they essentially told me that was as far as I'd ever go in the company.

I did become part of the strategic transition team the family put together to bring in the new leadership team. Hooray for me. The first step they took was to hire a new president from the outside. And as soon as they installed this new president, they backed away from the business and gave this individual a tremendous amount of autonomy. The owners formed an advisory group that met with the president on a quarterly basis to see how the business was performing—otherwise they were no longer involved in the day-to-day running of the business.

The very first thing the new president did was crack down on communications (as tyrants often do). He was extremely regimented in how he wanted communication to be handled, especially with the family ownership group. In his first week on the job, he made a direct "request" of me: never speak to the family again. That was quite a blow; I had developed a close and trusting relationship with the family over sixteen years of working with them, so to cut off all communication with them felt wrong. In case I hadn't gotten the message, the president pulled me aside a few days after taking office and said, "I am here to make money. Anyone who stands in my way won't be here any longer. Do I make myself clear?"

I knew in that moment that this person's leadership style was going to be detrimental to the growth of the company. If he was willing to be so openly antagonistic to me—a valuable long-term member of the management team—I knew his arrogant, dictatorial, money-driven style would carry across all of his other dealings as well. I braced myself; we were in for a rocky ride.

This man was highly intelligent, and he knew finances quite well. He could read a P&L statement with the best of them, and he was terrific at analyzing spreadsheets and projecting numbers. He knew, just by going over all our documents and data, which areas of the company he wanted to target in order to improve the business. There was only one minor problem: he didn't understand our *business* at all. All he understood was abstract analytics.

In our industry, everyone has injection-molding machines, everyone buys raw materials, and everyone does designs and engineering. The differentiator in making a business successful is the people you have in your company. If you don't treat your people as your most important asset, you won't have them much longer. They won't be loyal to you, and they won't work hard for you. And when you go into battle, they won't be standing by your side.

It very quickly became clear to me that this man did not care about people at all. Which meant, to me, that he didn't understand our business at its core. I actually said those exact words to him on many occasions: "You don't understand our business." And this would drive him into apoplexy; he needed to believe he was the smartest person in the room.

Because people weren't important to him, he didn't understand or value the company culture—a business's most important intangible asset—and he didn't understand why we were in the business we were. He didn't understand what drove us, what incentivized us, what rewarded us. He didn't understand what had made us successful, or how we had gained the customers we had, so he didn't know how to gain or keep customers going forward. To win business, it's critical that you understand your unique value proposition. What is a UVP? It's the people, processes, products, and innovations you present as a package to your customers in order to tell them, "We want to work with you, and we're going to warrant your business."

He didn't *get* our UVP. Customers were simply numbers on a page to him, and so were employees.

The president's disrespectful, people-last attitude caused him to alienate employees in all areas of the company. He treated the engineers, designers, and tech people dismissively. So they began walking out the door, taking all of their technological know-how and design knowledge with them. He insulted the sales staff on the front end by the way he chose to compensate them, and so they began leaving, too, taking all their customer relationships with them. Human resources became a revolving door. Before long, we'd lost so many good people we couldn't design our way out of a paper bag, and we didn't have relationships with any of our customers.

The president also had his own private business model that he used for quoting products and coming up with pricing—and his pricing just wasn't competitive in the industry. So basically, we found ourselves with no engineering, no customer relationships, and poor pricing. Three strikes and ... you know the drill.

For the last three years of my employment with this company, I had to watch this president and his antics destroy a wonderful company that I and other good people had built for the last two decades. And I had to watch people I cared about being marginalized, having their accomplishments negated, and losing their livelihoods. This company was in a very small town, so the people who were terminated had no other employment opportunities, unless they wanted to pack up and leave their hometown. It was a true tragedy. (By the way, the company recently sold for pennies on the dollar, a shell of its former self.)

The saddest part was knowing that if I had been in charge, none of this would have happened. That's not arrogance speaking; it's just the truth. The experience was truly dispiriting.

The longer I stayed there, the worse I felt. I had given my loyalty, my energy, and the biggest part of my life to this company, and for what? It was bad enough to have been passed over for the head job—knowing I had what it took to excel in the position—but it was infinitely worse to watch all the value I had created being trashed.

Finally, I'd had enough. I was ready for something new. And I made a solemn vow to myself: "If I ever get the opportunity to lead a business, I'm going to build it on the right foundation."

OPPORTUNITY KNOCKS

During the time all this was going on, I received a call from a colleague of mine who said, "Hey, Doug, there's someone I think you might want to meet with next time you're in the area. He's an older gentleman, and he owns a small company; you might want to hear him out."

I finally arranged to meet this guy over lunch, and he told me he owned a smallish—$8–$10 million—injection-molding company in Saline, Michigan. "Here's the deal," he said to me as we sat down to eat. "I'm eighty years old, and I'm looking to get out of the business." He was living in Florida most of the time, he explained, flying back and forth to Michigan, as needed, to check in on the company. And he was tired. He wasn't really interested in selling the company; he was trying to create a succession plan so he could retire completely. As we wrapped up our meal, he said, "Why don't you let me show you the place?"

The minute I walked in the door of MMI Engineered Solutions, I felt like I was stepping back in time. The place reminded me of what my current nineteen-year employer had looked like back when I'd joined it as a young man after leaving General Motors.

The first thing I wanted to do that day was walk around and get an unvarnished, firsthand look at the place. I wanted to watch the people. How did they interact? What was the look on their faces? What was the culture like? How were things organized?

Just by walking around a plant, I can size up a company pretty quickly. Are they organized? Do they have good quality processes in place? Are their products complex? *Too* complex? Are the products unique, or are they commodity-type products everyone knows how to make? Is there a flow to product operations? Do they have a one-man show with one guy doing everything? Is the furniture old and decrepit? Are people's desks messy, piled with old junk? How do people talk to each other? What's the energy level?

Immediately, I knew I was looking at a rudderless ship. I could see that the plant was not well organized. I noticed people walking around who … let's just say, they didn't have Christmas-morning smiles on their faces. There was no sense of direction. No one was vying for Employee of the Month—or even Employee of the Hour. I looked at the way their work cells were put together, and there weren't a lot of efficiencies. There was zero evidence of a positive, cooperative culture.

When I sat down in the office with members of the management team, it was clear there were no policies and procedures in place, nothing written down, no documented processes. All of the operations details were being carried around in people's heads.

There was no growth in the company either. Their financial performance was poor. No one seemed to know whether the company was competitive or not. Or where it made money. Or *why* it made money. There was no visible strategy. There were obvious areas where they could increase their margins, but no one was taking advantage.

In short, the company was a hot mess. I was thrilled beyond belief. Thrilled? Yes, because I could see a hundred ways I could add value to this enterprise, and I could do so quickly.

I looked at their customer base and said to myself, "Wow, they've got some pretty sizable customers, but they don't have any penetration." Turned out, they had *twelve salespeople*—a huge sales staff for such a small company—but each one was selling very little, because they were calling on a dozen industries in a scattered and superficial way. As a team, they were trying to be a jack-of-all-trades, instead of master of a few.

They didn't know which customers they were calling on, with which products, and why. They didn't know how to quote products.

Oh, and there was rampant nepotism too.

In short, the company was a hot mess.

I was thrilled beyond belief.

Thrilled? Yes, because I could see a hundred ways I could add value to this enterprise, and I could do so quickly. We were a perfect match in that sense. They were a rudderless ship in need of a captain; I was a captain in need of a vessel.

And it wasn't as if the company was a hopeless case. There *was* potential here—serious potential, in the right hands—but that potential simply was not being realized.

What were the pluses? Well, for one thing, the engineering staff had some serious chops. I met with a few of the engineers and learned there were three of them who each had a minimum of twenty-eight years of tenure. These guys knew their products well and had legitimate skills, but no one was managing or directing them. They were an untapped resource.

Customer-wise, while it was true that the company had poor sales penetration, it did have some good customers and, more importantly, it had *supplier codes* with these customers. Once you have a supplier code, you are in a customer's supply base, which means you essentially have an open invitation to work with them. It's no small feat to get a supplier code to work with a large automotive OEM (original equipment manufacturer).

The attribute that excited me the most, however, was the fact that they had their own in-house tool shop, where they designed and built their own injection-molding tools ("tool" is the industry term for a mold). This was a unique feature for an injection-molding plant. I knew it could be a huge factor in putting together a value proposition. You see, most injection molders buy their molds outside the company. And nowadays everyone buys these tools out of China, because they're cheaper than anywhere else. But there are drawbacks to dealing with China—time delays being chief among them.

With an in-house tool shop, we could tell our customers, "We can build our own tooling for your products, and we can do it faster and cheaper than anyone else, including China." Which would mean better prices and faster turnaround for the customer.

I believed I could take the fundamentals that were in place—a good basic injection-molding technology, an in-house tool shop, and a great customer base to which I would now have access—and combine them with my product knowledge, people management skills, and understanding of customer satisfaction, to create a thriving enterprise. To say I was excited about the possibilities would be like saying Phoenix is a little warm in the summer.

I sat down with the owner again, and I told him, "Look, if I'm going to come in on this, I don't want to just be the president. I want to own the company. If we can work out an arrangement where I can come in and lead the company with a deal on the table to do an acquisition, I'm interested."

Long story short, we figured out a way to do it. I was ready to dive in with both feet.

TAKING STOCK

Taking the reins of MMI Engineered Solutions was the opportunity I'd been preparing for my whole professional life. Before I jumped in, though, I wanted to step back for a moment and take stock of where I had been and where I wanted to go. I was determined to do this right. I thought back on everything that had gone wrong at my old company. I thought about everything I had learned in all my years in business and education. And I thought about what needed to be done to turn this new company around.

> *I knew that if I had to distill all the lessons I'd learned, in all of my business experiences, down to one sentence I could use to guide me, it would be this: Business is people.*

I revisited the commitment I had made to myself that if I ever had a chance to run my own company, I would build it on the right foundation. So what *was* that right foundation? I didn't have to think about it very hard. I knew that if I had to distill all the lessons I'd learned, in all of my business experiences, down to one sentence I could use to guide me, it would be this:

Business is people.

People are the beginning, middle, and end of every business. Without the people, there is no business. Business is not about P&L statements, cost efficiencies, organizational charts, or even products and services. It's about human beings. I knew that if I really wanted to succeed at this opportunity, I would need to listen to, respect, care about, focus on, and strive to understand the people. If I did that, then succeed or fail, I would know I had given it my best effort.

And that's what I want you to understand, more than any other idea in this book. If you want to own and/or lead a thriving organization, you must put people first. Period. End of discussion.

Before starting my first day at MMI, I remade that commitment to myself. I vowed that I would treat this new business as a human enterprise, every single day.

And that meant taking a fresh look at the people at every level of the company …

EMPLOYEES

Your number one assets as a businessperson are the people who work for you. And so you must treat them as such. You must respect them, talk to them, get to know them, and treat them as you would want to be treated. But before you even do that, you need to make sure you have the right people on your team. If you don't hire the right people, put them in the right places, and organize them in the right manner, you won't even make it out of the starting gate. I knew that would be job one.

The most challenging task, especially when you inherit an existing workforce, is to get people's minds right. They need to be focused and have the right attitude. I use a phrase all the time: "If the mind is right, the body will follow." A pretty simple statement, but it says a lot. Just because people nod their head and say, "Yeah, okay, I'm on board," doesn't mean they really are.

A big challenge I faced immediately at MMI was that employees had no sense of the big picture. They didn't know which customers were important to us, they didn't know which products were important to us, and they didn't know whether the company was performing well. They just knew that they had a job to come to every day, and if they weren't doing something correctly, someone would yell at them and tell them what to do. They had no idea whether what they were doing was successful or whether they were even important in the company.

I believe it is critical that people know why their position is important, how it fits into the overall plan, and how their performance affects the company. They should be able to quickly answer questions such as: How is the company doing today? How have we done in the past? What is our approach going forward, and why? A big part of my job would be to teach, coach, and mentor employees so that they could not only answer these questions but use their answers to motivate them on a daily basis.

Beyond how you treat people as individuals, you also need to have the right culture—a culture of cooperation, communication, transparency, pride, purpose. We'll devote a whole chapter to culture later in the book, but this was an area I knew I'd have to tackle right away.

Finally, something that became clear to me as I assumed the reins of this company is that each employee has people—families—who depend on them. These people are important too. Today, for example, I have two hundred direct employees, and each one of them, on average, has a four-person family. That means I'm affecting eight hundred people and their livelihoods with the decisions I make every day. And I need to be sure these additional people can be successful and stable too.

MANAGEMENT/LEADERSHIP TEAM

Your most important employees, of course, are the members of your leadership team. They are the ones who will be working alongside you to ensure that your vision for the company is executed faithfully on an ongoing basis. They are the ones who will share the teaching, coaching, and mentoring responsibilities with you. It is vital that you have open, honest, and trusting relationships with all the members of your management and leadership teams.

My experience with my previous employer had shown me what can happen when company executives and ownership are not communicating effectively about their mutual goals and are not on the same page. I vowed never to let the same thing happen on my watch.

As the leader of a company, you can't guarantee every manager and executive will find ultimate career satisfaction in your company. Sometimes people need to move on. But what you *can* do is have open and transparent communications with them. This means getting to know the *person*, not just the role they fill. I promised myself I would do that.

CUSTOMERS

Your customers are nearly as important to you as your team members. It's crucial to remember, at all times, that your customers are not numbers on a spreadsheet; they are living, breathing human beings with desires they want fulfilled. And if you don't go out of your way to find out what their desires are, someone else will. Customers are not a given. They owe you nothing. You must treat them with honor, gratitude, and respect, or you will lose them, sooner or later.

If you can't articulate what your value proposition is to the customers you want to serve, you're not ready to be a business owner. And the only way to do that is to take the time to get to know your customers as people.

That's why I vowed to myself that I would devote a lot of time, when I first started at the company, to visiting my customers in person. I would be candid with them about who I was, and I would ask them to be candid with me. I would go to each of them and say, "This is who I am, and I'd love your honest feedback about what you think of us as a company. Are we doing a good job? A poor job? Let me have it with both barrels."

I vowed I would be grateful for whatever feedback they gave me, good or bad—especially the bad—and I would use it to create a new value proposition for the company.

THE COMMUNITY

Your focus on people doesn't stop at the edge of the company parking lot. One thing I had learned early, in my MBA classes, is that you cannot be a successful leader in an industry unless you give back to your community. You must take whatever level of success you've had and share it with people who aren't as fortunate. I intended to honor that responsibility as a leader too. I would strive to have a real effect on the lives of the real people who made up our community.

YOURSELF

And finally, there's one person you can't ignore as you go forward as a business owner, and that is yourself (and your family). As we discussed earlier, you need to define success for yourself and make sure your personal goals and the goals of the business are aligned. You need to continually grow and improve your skills and knowledge so that you're giving the business the best you possibly can. You must also ensure that the business is on track to fulfill all the requirements of your definition of success. Ideally, the relationship between you and your business should be a love affair in which you mutually serve one another. But that can only happen if the two "lovers" remain compatible. That requires continual self-awareness and self-knowledge on your part. I promised myself I would always strive for that.

* * *

Once you're crystal clear about the importance of people to your business, *that's* when you can dig in and start moving pieces around. I was now ready to do that at MMI. And for me, I knew it was going to mean taking the business apart and putting it back together again...

CHAPTER 2

BREAKING IT DOWN, PUTTING IT BACK TOGETHER

I believed in the potential of MMI Engineered Solutions—or I wouldn't have become involved—but that potential was purely theoretical at the time I came aboard. The company was a rudderless ship. I described some of its issues in the last chapter—a disengaged workforce, unhappy customers, a lack of product focus, poor workflow, constant turnover, and an EBITDA (earnings before interest, taxes, depreciation, and amortization) fluctuating between zero profitability and single digits, to name just a very few.

Amazon it wasn't.

But no one seemed to be thinking about what the company should be doing differently. Everyone seemed resigned to the status quo.

Changing this company was going to be a massive undertaking. But one thing I had learned in my engineering education was that when you first look at a problem—any problem, in any area of life—it can often seem complex and overwhelming. The only way to achieve the outcome you desire is to break the problem down into its smallest pieces, create a plan for each of the pieces, and then put things back together. That was the job I was going to need to do here. I believed I was up to the challenge; I'd been training for this opportunity for years and was raring to go. But was everyone else up to the challenge? That was the X factor.

THE VALUE PROPOSITION

When you take the reins of a company, any company, the first thing you do is "punt"—buy yourself a little time to figure things out. That's what I did at MMI. I didn't yet know what our assets and capabilities were. The only thing I knew for sure was what we *didn't* have: a clear value proposition. And that was where I needed to focus first.

Your value proposition is the heart and soul of your business. Without it, you don't *have* a business. A value proposition is the answer to the question, "What can we uniquely offer to customers, and why will they want to come to *us* instead of our competitors?" Identifying and committing to your value proposition is job one. And as I said before, when I'm thinking about a VP, my aim is to create a mutual dynamic whereby my customers value me and I value my customers. Both aspects are important.

We didn't have that at MMI. And I needed to figure out why, pronto. I immediately went to work on both sides of the equation: us and our customers. I started with our management team and set up regular one-on-one meetings with them. Where was the business heading? How did they think the company was performing? Their departments? What were their ideas about how to improve things? I talked to our customers, too, in person. People first, remember?

I quickly began to see that we had problems on both sides of the value equation. In some cases, we had customers we weren't valuing but should have been. In other cases, we had customers we were valuing *too* highly: customers that weren't really good for us …

UNDERVALUED CUSTOMERS

When I talked to our customers, I heard a lot of things that didn't make me want to dance the happy dance, things like: "Your people don't hold their promises." "You're late on your deliveries." "You nickel and dime us to death with your pricing." When you hear the same type of thing from many different sources, you know you have a foundational problem, and if you don't fix it, your days are numbered.

Our communication as a company was notoriously poor. We'd tell customers, "Five weeks from now, you'll have your parts," and then we'd miss the date. Two days after the deadline, the customer would call *us* and say, "Hey, you guys were supposed to ship us parts. Where are they?" And we'd say, "Oh, yeah, we're going to be late on those."

That, in case you're wondering, is not how you show customers you value them.

There was one particular gentleman I went to see—a manager at a company that *should have been* a highly valued customer of ours. He stood out in particular because he was such a forthright and candid individual. He was also a guy who had clearly developed a very negative attitude toward us. We'll call him Jim. He looked me in the eye and said, "I've seen a lot of guys from your company come in here and ask for feedback. And I tell them exactly what our complaints are, and then nothing changes. So I don't believe you'll make any changes, either, but I'll tell you exactly what I think: your costs are out of control, you don't deliver product on time, you fail to meet your commitments, and I don't think I can do a lot of work with you going forward because I don't trust you'll do a good job for me."

Well, then.

I took Jim's words to heart, and he became symbolically important to me. I knew that if we could turn *him* around—which would be really tough, given his attitude—we would have gone a long way toward turning our entire company around. I vowed to pay especially close attention to Jim's products and projects. We would prove to Jim that we valued him, and he would come to value us. That was my personal promise.

I also noted a negative attitude among our own management toward certain customers, which seemed misplaced. For example, one of the first things the owner asked me to do when I first took the reins was to "get rid of" General Motors as a customer, because they were seen as a problem. This was painful for me to hear, because of my family's deep connection to GM, but it also seemed objectively crazy. With a company as big and respected as GM, there should be endless opportunity to do business. You don't just walk away from that. I also knew that when you lose a big institutional customer like GM, it's almost impossible to win them back. I said to the then owner, "Can you give me a little time with GM? Let me figure out why we have problems there and see if we can turn them into a valued customer."

"OVERVALUED" CUSTOMERS

On the other side of the coin, our company was devoting enormous resources to certain customers, where our investment clearly wasn't justified. As an example of this, one of our sales guys had made inroads with an aerospace company that was converting a rudder control system for an aircraft from metal to plastic. There were eighteen different metal pieces that needed to be converted, and we were working on developing the project.

We had multiple designers and multiple engineers assigned to this beast. It was like a black hole of resources. For starters, the requirements to work with an aerospace program are steep. You need something called an AS9100 certification. This requires tons of quality checks and audits, which translates to a lot of people and a lot of man-hours spent jumping through hoops. Our manufacturing costs were huge too. When we would run one of the special tools to make a few sample pieces, it would take days—even weeks—to make the parts, tying up our production capacity. And if you looked at the dollars that could be generated by this project, it was maybe a couple of hundred thousand dollars a year. This was nuts.

The team was spending so much time developing this set of products, it was paralyzing the company. And nobody was telling anybody to stop! When I saw the resources that were being poured into pursuing this one piece of business, my jaw hit the ground. The capital requirements were literally going to bankrupt the company.

One major drawback was that the people working on the project had no real idea what they were doing, because they had no grounding in the aerospace industry. So they'd had to invest a ton of time in getting up to speed on a whole industry—just to do one low-ticket job! And nobody in leadership was saying, "Why are we doing this? We're not a charity organization. Does this business fit our technology and know-how, and can we make money at this?"

Luckily, our teams had kept some records of all the time we had been spending on the project. So I went to visit that customer and said, "Look, I respect your business, and I'd love to work with you, but until we get paid for the engineering and development work we've done so far, we're not doing any more work on this. I'm sorry, but we're not a free engineering service."

Eventually we were able to transition the client to another manufacturer, and we were paid the money we were owed—about $700,000. So we came out okay in the end, but this was a clear example of a customer we *did not need* as a business.

CUTTING THROUGH THE NOISE

The only way we were going to have a viable value proposition was if our customers were important to us and we were important to them. A two-way street. And the only way that was going to happen was if (1) *we* were operating in areas that maximized our core skills, and (2) we were pursuing customers who could bring us profitable and sustained business.

So how would we get there? The situation at the company was extremely "noise-filled" at the time. Our attention was scattered in so many different directions, it was hard to get a focused sense of strategy and purpose. It didn't take me long to diagnose the root cause of the problem: our sales strategy (or lack thereof).

As I mentioned, we had twelve salespeople, way too many for a company our size. And they were trolling for business in far too many areas. We were trying to be a jack-of-all-trades, going after customers in areas as diverse as aerospace, medical, toys, food packaging, military, heavy trucks, material handling, and industrial automation. What would typically happen is that we'd land scattered accounts in these industries, but we didn't have *expertise* in most of them. So we were spending too much to get these accounts, and then we weren't delivering the know-how, quality, and service needed to make us a valued, go-to supplier.

Too much of our work was nonrenewable, and that was affecting our overall quality. We'd land a one-off job, ramp up our staff to complete that job, and then let people go when the job was done. There was too much employee turnover, not enough continuity. As a result, we didn't have a tenured, well-trained, and emotionally invested workforce. We did have *some* steady, renewable business, but not enough of it. We needed to increase this renewable business so that our earnings would be stable enough to retain staff through the ups and downs of the nonrenewable business. The way to do that would be to find the right customers.

After studying our core competencies—in engineering, design, manufacturing, etc.—and looking at our deepest and most promising customer markets, I concluded that there were two areas, and two areas only, that ought to represent our core business going forward: heavy trucks and custom-molded material handling products.

A little background on these:

Heavy trucks. These are the big rigs. A couple of decades ago, there was nothing luxurious about the cab of a Class 8 eighteen-wheeler. That situation started to change in the new millennium, to the point where the interiors of today's truck cabs look like the cockpits of private jets. But the industry faced some challenges in getting from there to here. You see, unlike Ford or GM, which make millions of cars a year, these truck companies make only tens of thousands of vehicles per year. Which meant that the volume for each of the interior parts they needed was too low for them to afford expensive injection-mold tooling. So they had to use thermoformed or formed-metal parts, which weren't very high in quality. Here's where our in-house tool shop revealed its value. We found a way to develop the tooling at a very low cost. So we could say to the manufacturer, essentially, "We can make your low-volume parts at a high quality, so your truck cabs can have the fit and finish of a Lexus." Now *that's* a value proposition. And that was the birth of our heavy-truck business—where I hoped much of our renewable business would come from.

Material handling. The automotive industry uses billions of manufactured components. The packaging costs for shipping these parts to the car manufacturers can be enormous. So instead of shipping a part—say, a water pump—in a cardboard box that gets used only once and thrown away, you make a plastic composite box, molded to fit that specific part, and you reuse that container again and again for as long as the vehicle is being made. When it comes to shipping critical engine and transmission parts, these fitted containers need to be highly engineered products. They require a lot of technology and know-how to make them properly and cost effectively. We had several engineers on staff who were very good at this, so I said to myself, "I can leverage those engineering resources, and we can do well in that industry."

So that was going to be our whole business. Two areas of focus, not a dozen. Two areas where we could offer high value and expertise rather than stumbling competency.

I proceeded to break up our sales department, letting go of eight of our twelve salespeople. Of the remaining four, I divided them up, two per industry. So although we were cutting our sales staff by two-thirds, we were actually doubling it in the two areas we wanted to go after.

With this move, most of the company noise was effectively silenced. We could now focus on creating and delivering a value proposition that we all understood and believed in. At least that was the plan.

A NEW STANDARD

Next we needed to fix everything we were doing wrong. Our customers were continually telling us we were messing up. Our response was always to promise to do better next time. But then we'd rinse and repeat. I realized the problem came down to the fact that we had no internal standards. There was nothing guiding our performance. And so I came up with a new standard for the company:

At the foundation of everything we do, there are three areas we will always focus on: *(1) we will create a quality product, (2) we will deliver it on time, and (3) we will do it at a competitive price.* Every single policy, procedure, strategy, and design/engineering decision would center on those three things. We would start and finish every project with those three criteria in mind.

Simplicity is the key when setting standards. If you come up with eight criteria you need to hit, no one will be able to remember them. You need a standard that is simple to keep in mind though challenging to execute. And you need to stress that standard over and over again—in meetings, in printed materials, in one-on-one communications—until it becomes engrained in people's minds and in the culture. We'll talk about that more, later in the book.

QUALITY

Okay, we had our three-part standard. Now I needed to break those three components down even further and get specific. Starting with quality, I said to myself, "What do we need to do, every day, to ensure quality?"

One step would be to narrow our company's focus, which I described above. That would go a long way to improving our quality. But there were several other key areas that needed work:

When I think about product flow in any manufacturing plant, I use the model of a marble in a shoebox. That is, you put a marble in one side, you tilt the box the other way, and the marble rolls straight to the other side. That's the kind of product flow you want. Direct, clean, fast, intuitive.

A MARBLE IN A SHOEBOX

I went through our whole physical plant with a critical eye. I asked myself, "Are we set up for producing quality products?" Answer: no, we weren't. I essentially had to "blow everything up" and start over from scratch. I realized we had a bunch of old capital equipment that was inefficient and had a lot of downtime on it, so I made arrangements to replace that equipment. Then I asked, "What would an efficient product flow look like in my plant?"

When I think about product flow in any manufacturing plant, I use the model of a marble in a shoebox. That is, you put a marble in one side, you tilt the box the other way, and the marble rolls straight to the other side. That's the kind of product flow you want. Direct, clean, fast, intuitive. You don't want the marble zigging and zagging or getting stuck in the middle or needing to be manually carried to a different part of the box. So I started to move things around the plant, completely reorganizing things to achieve a good product flow.

SAFE, CLEAN, AND ORGANIZED

I also began to implement a lesson I had learned years earlier: you need to be safe, clean, and organized before you can even *start* talking about quality. So we began to comb through the plant, removing hazards, cleaning up messes, and reorganizing work stations in practical ways. We instituted new policies and procedures in all these areas—including a policy of starting every new discussion with the topic of safety, which we still do today.

THE RIGHT QUALIFIERS

Quality needs to be a given when you're talking to your customer base, and one of the ways you establish that is by attaining top industry certifications. In our industry at the time, that meant getting our TS 16949 certification, which I immediately set out to do. To receive the TS 16949 stamp of approval, you hire an independent auditor who comes in and does an extensive examination of every aspect of your business. If you meet their standards, they give you a plaque and a certification, which goes a long way toward qualifying you as a supplier for the customers we go after.

We also went after our ISO 14001 certification for being environmentally friendly. Not only was this the right thing to do, but it would also appeal to environmentally conscious customers.

TIMING

Timing was the second part of our standard. We needed to change our staff's mind-set in this area. Late deliveries could no longer be an accepted business practice. Completion dates needed to be baked into our employees' minds. For that reason, I implemented a policy, which we still adhere to today, that no meeting may take place *on any topic* that does not have a concrete time frame associated with it. Why? Because if you come in and talk about any sort of initiative or task and you don't have a completion date, your team will never move at the pace you need. I don't care if you're talking about a finance task, a design challenge, a sales goal, or delivering or costing a product—you need to have timing tied to it. *Then*, and only then,

In an ideal work environment, there should be a crisp sort of cadence you can feel in the air, an energy. We didn't have that at MMI. One of my most important and immediate tasks was to set a new cadence for the company.

can you focus your attention on actually *being* on time.

PRICING

Finally, we needed to get our pricing right. I spent a lot of time looking at our pricing models to understand what our customers would bear for prices, and then I compared these prices to what we were actually charging. I found a lot of variance. In some cases, we were charging for things we didn't need to charge for (which was making us noncompetitive); in other cases, it was clear that customers would pay a lot *more* for things we weren't charging them for. We were leaving a lot of money on the table, simply because no one had bothered to understand what our competition was doing, pricing-wise, and what the market would pay for our products. Those days were over. From now on, we would be experts on our market.

SETTING A CADENCE: THE VALUE OF COMMUNICATION AND METRICS

One of the most "broken" aspects of MMI when I came aboard was its work cadence. You could tell, just from the rhythm of the plant, that workers were not meaningfully engaged with the work they were doing or the final outcomes. People were just showing up and doing what was required in order to avoid being yelled at. In an ideal work environment, there should be a crisp sort of cadence you can feel in the air, an energy. We didn't have that at MMI. One of my most important and immediate tasks was to set a new cadence for the company.

This was not a simple fix. I knew it was going to take two things: communication and metrics.

Communication, which I'll talk more about in future chapters, is critical to engaging and energizing your workforce. People need to fully understand the job they are working on, its importance to the company, and the way their job relates to other jobs and fits into the overall scheme of things. They also need feedback on what they need to do every day and how well they are doing it. That's where the importance of metrics comes in.

YOU GET WHAT YOU MEASURE

I'm a huge believer that you get what you measure. Any goal you want to achieve, you need to measure it, quantify it, and break it down into attainable performance units. This applies to sales goals, financial targets, labor efficiency, you name it. You need to turn your desired result into a set of metrics. You start with a macro view of where you need to be, and then you break that goal down into monthly, weekly, and daily performance. Once you know where the daily performance level needs to be, you can start to build a cadence around that.

Let's use a company's top-line number—its overall revenues—as an example. Say your goal is to be at $50 million for the year. You don't just wait till the end of the year and say, "Oops, we only made it to $40 million. We missed our goal." You break the goal number down into twelve months, and you say, "To reach our goal, we have to do a little over $4 million per month." I'm oversimplifying here to make a point, but that means you need to ship roughly $1 million in product a week. At five days a week, that's $200,000 a day. And if you're running three shifts, that means each shift needs to produce about $70,000 in product to stay on pace.

Knowing this target immediately sets the tone for the pace everyone needs to move at. You know how to attack your day; you know how fast you need to move, hour by hour, to meet your requirements; and at the end of the day, you know whether you've been successful or not. When you have a successful day, this helps you get to tomorrow and make tomorrow successful too. Then you start to string together a few successful days, which sets the tone for the week, which helps you meet your goal for the month, and then for the quarter. Cadence.

> **If you use the right metrics, you can see the entire heartbeat of a company on a single piece of paper.**

METRICS = EMPOWERMENT

If you use the right metrics, you can see the entire heartbeat of a company on a single piece of paper. That's why I began breaking every aspect of the business down into what I call corporate measurables—we'll talk about these in more detail later—and why we continue to work this way today. We create a metric for everything, and we assign an owner of that metric. And then we come together in a series of daily, weekly, and monthly meetings to track our progress. The owner of each metric comes to the meeting prepared to discuss whether they have met their goal or not, and why. If they've been successful, they also need to show whether their success is sustainable or not—we don't want to just get lucky.

Once a month we compare our performance to best-in-class metrics provided to us by a consulting firm to see if we're hitting our industry's top benchmarks. This is how we ensure high quality. We color the metric green, red, or yellow—green if you met best in class, red if you didn't, and yellow if you could have made it but didn't quite.

Using metrics is all about giving everyone the information and feedback they need to set a cadence for themselves and be successful on a day-to-day basis. One of the things I invested heavily in was an enterprise resource planning (ERP) software system that allows you to assign metrics to every aspect of your business—sales, raw materials, manufacturing, costs, invoicing—and slice and dice your business in a million ways. I then installed an eighty-inch screen in the middle of the plant, with all nineteen of our work cells displayed and color-coded. You can tell at a glance whether things are good or not in every area of the company. And then, at each work station there's a little iPad-like device. It's color-coded, too, and tells the operator, essentially, "You're going fast enough to hit the standard [or you're not]." Giving this information to workers puts the ownership of their work rhythm in their own hands, instead of having someone standing over them, yelling at them, which only creates tension.

The system sends us automated reports, too, that tell us ahead of time whether there are any red flags that might affect the on-time delivery of our products.

The whole system is highly interactive. It's regular and continuous with every employee at all levels of the company. And it all ties back to (1) quality, (2) timeliness, and (3) competitive pricing. Let's say, for example, we want to set a competitive price for a product, along with a level of profitability associated with that. If I quote the product to be made to a certain quality standard and I'm making it too slowly, that means I'm spending more money on it than I should be, which means my profitability will be compromised. The system lets us see that every step of the way.

* * *

So those were some of the main areas I focused on in my initial process of taking things apart and putting them back together. But I knew from experience that this didn't mean I had truly changed the company permanently and for the better. Real change takes time and sustained effort. "Change the mind, and the body will follow" is one of my guiding mottoes. And I knew *that* kind of change was going to be the most difficult change of all.

CHAPTER 3

BEING A CHANGE AGENT

O ne of the funniest stories I ever heard as a business leader was not meant to be funny at all. I was talking to a colleague of mine who had just come back from a whirlwind business trip. He had recently been hired by a global company, and his boss told him, "You need to work at changing the company culture in the area of quality."

This colleague took the mission to heart. He sat in his office and came up with a great plan for a quality-based culture. He then literally jumped on an airplane and flew to each of the company's plants around the world. He spent one day at each plant, delivering his presentation on quality-based culture and hanging inspiring signs and posters around each workplace.

I saw him shortly after his return, and he told me, "I feel really good about my trip. I changed the culture of our company with respect to quality, and now we're going to be in good shape going forward."

I was polite enough not to chuckle, but do you see why I said this was a funny story? You don't change a company's culture by

You must be the active carrier of the change. You must live it, think it, breathe it, speak it. Everything you do must embody the culture you are aiming for.

walking in the door for a day—as a complete stranger, no less—and *telling* people how you want them to think and behave. You change cultures over a long, *long* period of time. Did I mention *long?*

Individuals are resistant to change. Groups of people are even more resistant, and organizations are *exponentially* more so. The bigger a ship is, the harder it is to turn. To think you can change an organization quickly and permanently by waving a wand is like a teacher imagining she can change the behavior of an unruly class by writing "Quiet!" on the blackboard.

I've been at my company for seven years now, and we've made a lot of progress. But I know I still have a ton of work to do in creating positive change. If you talk to me seven years from now, I'll still have a ton of work to do. Change is a never-ending quest, not a one-shot deal.

In this chapter we'll talk about the challenge that organizational change represents. Change *is* possible—make no mistake about that—but only when you respect the enormity of the task.

CHANGE MUST BE LED

If you want change to occur at your company, you cannot *hope* for change or *order* people to change. You must lead the change. You must become the change agent. Being a change agent is not a one-day job, or a week-long job, or a month-long job. It is a permanent position. If you aim to see your organization improve in fundamental, long-term ways, you must, as Gandhi famously said, *be* the change you want to see. *You* must be the active carrier of the change. You must live it, think it, breathe it, speak it. Everything you do must embody the culture you are aiming for. You must be willing to push through resistance, again and again, and deal with negativity, disbelief, inertia, and apathy. If you can do that, the rewards can be enormous.

As I mentioned, when I started at MMI, people were taking bets around the water cooler on how long I'd last. Of course, no one told *me* that at the time. The only reason I know it now is that people eventually confided in me. Why? Because they saw results from the changes I was making and began to trust me. Now they tell me things like: "We've never seen anybody come into an organization and make the kinds of changes you've been able to make. You've taken this company to places we never thought it could go." The only reason I hear this kind of comment now is that I've been willing to *be* the change agent, day in and day out.

If you want to do the same, here are some fundamental guidelines to keep in mind …

RESPECT THE POWER OF COMFORT

The most crucial thing to understand when you come into an organization with change in mind is that comfort—inertia—is a massive force in the workplace. Human beings are creatures of habit. They set up their desks a certain way. They prioritize their tasks a certain way. They establish a habitual cadence in the way they work. When you come in and start making changes, people become uncomfortable. Massively so. And when human beings become uncomfortable, they either react defensively, or they smile in your face and then go right back to doing what they were doing before.

Comfort is a primal force, not just in human beings, but in all life forms. If you don't believe me, try to move a sleeping dog or cat. You might be needing stitches. One of the biggest fears people have when a change agent comes in is that they will never be comfortable again. And this triggers primal emotional reactions.

Know this: when you come in as the new change agent, you are perceived as an outsider and a threat to comfort. Even though you may now own the company, people's real allegiance is to their coworkers and to their own routines and habits, not to you. Take, for example, a front-line operator who has been doing his job for twenty years. When you tell him to start doing things differently, his attitude will be, "What does *this* guy know? He just showed up. I know my job better than he does. If there was a problem with my work, someone would have told me a long time ago." He might do the task your way once or twice, but as soon as you're not looking, he'll go back to doing it his way, because in his mind, he knows best.

Comfort may be a force of nature, but it is extremely dangerous to a business. Comfort allows people to become locked into their habits, for better or worse. They no longer care how their job affects other jobs in the company or the company as a whole; they only want to stay in their comfort zone. So, as a change agent, you need to make people *un*comfortable. The secret to doing that successfully is to have your eyes wide open. Understand that discomfort is going to trigger deep fears. *Anticipate* these fears, take them seriously, and be prepared to respond to them. Most of all, *communicate the reasons* for the changes. I tell people openly, "You're going to be very uncomfortable with these changes. But I will explain to you why we're doing them." If you can get people to understand and accept the rationale for the changes—and you can show them how they will benefit from those things—they will be much more likely to accept the discomfort.

A goal I have for my workforce is to make people "uncomfortably comfortable." By that I mean I don't want people to be complacently addicted to old, unproductive routines. I want them to be nimble and responsive to new ideas. On the other hand, I don't want them to be fearful and filled with anxiety every day. I want them to feel the workplace is a safe, inclusive, and accepting environment where they'll be treated fairly and respectfully as valued team members. Striking this balance between comfort and discomfort is critical.

ACTIVITY VERSUS PRODUCTIVITY

One of the keys to changing habitual behavior—and getting people past their discomfort—is to understand the difference between activity and productivity.

I remember an engineer once saying to me, "Sometimes I wish I had become a ditch digger. In the morning I could grab a shovel and start moving dirt from spot A to spot B. At the end of the day, I could point at my pile of dirt and say, 'I've been productive.' In my job I run around all day, and I'm busy, busy, busy. But when it's time to go home at five, I can't tell you what I got done."

This story epitomizes what I often see in the workplace. People become caught up in the routines and the minutiae of what they're doing, and they no longer recall what they're trying to accomplish. Because of this, they end up making the same mistakes over and over and behaving in absurdly inefficient ways. They've become attached to the activity, not the results.

As a leader, you must be fine-tuned to the difference between activity and productivity. You don't want anyone wasting time on activity that doesn't lead directly to productivity. You need to weed out habitual behavior that doesn't deliver value. That means you must constantly observe your managers and front-line staff and show them what it means to be productive rather than merely busy. You've probably heard of the 80–20 rule (or Pareto principle). In a work scenario, this says that 80 percent of our productivity comes from about 20 percent of our efforts. Your job is to identify those few tasks each employee does that lead to the greatest returns—and to prioritize *those* tasks instead of the low-return, time-filler stuff.

People actually *want* to be productive and to contribute. So when you are able to show them how a change in their work habits leads to greater output for the team and the company, they are usually willing to change their habits, and they'll start to buy in to your leadership approach.

COMMUNICATION IS EVERYTHING

One of the first things I noticed about MMI when I came aboard was that people didn't understand how their jobs related to other jobs in the company or to the success of the company. In our particular case, a lot of this was the result of the management style. I'm convinced the previous manager did not *want* his employees to know what was going on. He did not want the company to become more cohesive and productive. He preferred to keep it small and to keep employees in the dark because (I believe) he was afraid of losing control if the company became bigger and more successful.

The same sort of willful ignorance happens on the employee side too. Sometimes we don't *want* to know how our job relates to the company as a whole. We're afraid of the added responsibility. If we knew how our job was affecting the productivity of other teams and the company as a whole, we might be impelled to change the way we do things. And we don't want to change. So we'd rather keep the blinders on.

As a leader, you need to tackle this situation head-on. It's extremely vital that every employee know exactly how their job relates to other jobs in the company, how it affects the work and deadlines of other teams, and how it contributes to the success of the company. Sometimes you need to give people this knowledge even if they don't want to receive it.

In my company there is regular and continuous communication about what we're trying to achieve as a company and how every single employee contributes to that. We have daily meetings, weekly meetings, and monthly meetings in which we constantly talk about this. Performance reviews are an important aspect of this—every employee knows how they're contributing but also knows how they're expected to improve.

> *Transparency in communication is hugely important when trying to change a company. You want people to know your vision for the company, your goals, and your plans. You want everyone in the company to understand why you're making every change you make.*

Transparency in communication is hugely important when trying to change a company. You want people to know your vision for the company, your goals, and your plans. You want everyone in the company to understand why you're making every change you make. Remember, change stirs up fear, and if you don't tell people exactly why you're making a change, they will create their own story about it—a fear-based story. You need to get out in front of the storytelling machine and *be the storyteller*.

As a change agent, you need people to come along with you and help carry the torch for you. And the only way that will happen is if they believe in your message. So you have to articulate that message via regular, continuous communication. Hourly, daily, weekly, monthly, yearly.

YOUR ROLE IS NOT DICTATOR

How you communicate is as crucial as *what* you communicate. I am constantly amazed at how many would-be change agents believe that ordering people around is an effective way to get people to change. Ordering people to change doesn't work. Intimidating people into changing doesn't work. Belittling people doesn't work. You might achieve some short-term results by these methods, but you will pay a price down the road.

I'm a big subscriber to Stephen Covey's notion that you must seek to understand before you try to be understood. That doesn't happen when you talk down to people or try to use them as pawns to further your agenda. Instead you must *listen* first. Really listen. Find out what matters to your people. Find out what they think and feel about their job. Find out what they hope for. Find out what they struggle with. Ask for their ideas. Most people in supervisory roles are far more interested in getting others to listen to *them*. But if you start by listening and attempting to understand your staff, you will create a human bond that you can build on.

Be open, be accessible, be available. Don't lock yourself in a closed office all day long. One of the greatest compliments I've ever received was when an employee recently said in a survey, "I like management because they're approachable." When people find you approachable, they will confide in you, pointing out flaws in your process and giving you other invaluable intelligence from the front lines. When you manage by intimidation, people hunker down in their foxholes, afraid that if they stick their head out, it will be lopped off.

Not only must *you* be an open communicator, but you must also ensure that everyone on your management team is capable of communicating in an open, respectful style. Some people just aren't. I've had to fire managers because they ruled by intimidation or by cursing people out and were incapable of being trained otherwise. You can easily spot these people in an organization—the tension level rises as soon as they walk into the room. If someone on your management team is creating tension and fear, they must be dealt with.

DEAL WITH NEGATIVE INFLUENCERS EARLY

All negative influences in your company must be rooted out as early as possible. In virtually every organization, there are people who hinder growth, either actively or passively, by virtue of their negativity. Some of these are the naysayer types who embrace the word *impossible*. Others will nod and agree with you when you're talking to them and then proceed to ignore everything you said, undermining your efforts with their passive-aggressive attitudes. Then there are those who simply project negative energy, in their voices, their faces, their postures.

When I started at MMI, there were two people in high management positions who were extremely negative individuals. I quickly began to think of them as cancers in the organization. That's not too strong a word for it. Negative people need to be converted or removed before their negativity can eat away at the core of what you're trying to accomplish.

I believe in giving everyone a chance, but experience has taught me you can't give a persistently negative person too much rope. Talk to them, make it clear to them what they need to change, and then observe them closely. Notice whether their behavior alters. If it doesn't, deal with them decisively. You can sometimes influence a person who hasn't fully "gone over to the dark side," but for those who are really entrenched in their negativity, the only thing you can do is cut them loose. Yes, fire them. The sooner, the better. Sounds harsh, but there is no place for negative people in a positively changing company.

SET THE TONE AND CADENCE YOURSELF

As a leader and change agent, you must rise above all negative influences and set the positive tone and the cadence you want your team members to adopt. By being unfailingly positive, you might be looked upon as an amusing alien species at first, but as you begin to see results, you will win people over.

I had an important experience with this when I joined MMI. One of the deeply negative people I mentioned above was the head of engineering. I told him I wanted to quote a certain type of job to a prospective customer, and he said, "Why are you quoting them that product? We're not competitive in that area. The customer will never give us that business."

I replied, "Humor me. Let's just go down the path, play it out, see how it goes. Whatever happens, we'll learn something." He sighed and threw his hands up.

We went down the path, and we ended up winning that business. The engineering head was flabbergasted, but I told him, "I did my part; I landed the business. Now you make sure we engineer the tools correctly and get the product out the door on time and on budget. That's your job." As we rolled out production, I was personally on the tool-shop floor every day watching those tools being made and telling everyone, "Here's the due date. We've *got* to have this tool finished. We cannot be late." I had my sleeves rolled up and was working alongside my toolmakers, trying to understand the challenges they had and helping them deal with any obstacles that stood in the way of getting this job done on time.

This project ended up becoming a rallying point for my people—a major stepping-stone—and I gained a lot of credibility. How? By not being the guy sitting in an office barking out orders. I was out there on the floor setting the cadence myself. When we succeeded in delivering the job and gaining a satisfied customer, we had living proof that change is possible.

> *Modeling is everything. You must embody the cadence, energy, and commitment you are asking your team to adopt. And you must never let up.*

Modeling is everything. *You* must embody the cadence, energy, and commitment you are asking your team to adopt. And you must never let up. If your direct reports or front-line people detect even one note of falsehood in you or suspect you're just mouthing business platitudes, you will lose them. But if you keep up a committed cadence and let your conviction shine in your eyes, your energy will eventually become infectious, and others will come aboard.

CONFLICT AVERSION

One of the biggest obstacles to change in an organization is fear of conflict. This fear exists at every level. Front-line workers don't want to create conflict with their coworkers or bosses. Bosses don't want to create conflict with tenured workers. No one wants to have a tense meeting in which they're critical of someone else in the company—this creates stress, and no one wants to be looked upon as the person causing that stress. So people will avoid conflict, almost at all costs, allowing detrimental conditions to persist.

Unless you are willing to confront this fear of conflict and look it in the eye, it will undermine much of the change you hope to accomplish.

To be a change agent, you must *welcome* conflict. Conflict is a good thing because it brings organizational and personnel problems to light so they can be solved. But you must be sure to handle conflict in a constructive way. First you must create an atmosphere—through your words and actions—in which people feel safe to deal openly with conflict and they know they won't get their heads bitten off. That takes time; it does not happen overnight.

Second, you must be sure to treat everyone the same way and be absolutely fair. If possible, try to handle conflicts in a group setting without singling anyone out. Don't call out one individual without calling out everyone who plays a part in the issue at hand.

Assure people you're with them, not against them. Try to remove any sense of implicit threat. Say something like, "You're not on the verge of losing your jobs. We're talking about this issue because we all want continuous improvement. And we all need to be working together toward that goal. Everyone needs to be on board, and everyone needs to understand their role and responsibility in this change process."

If you do need to speak to a particular individual, bring them into your office. Tell them, "I could have called you out in front of the whole team, but I didn't want to do that to you. However, I *am* holding you responsible for this, and I am asking you to change. So what's it going to be? Are you with me? Are you going to adopt these changes?"

Try to depersonalize issues. One way to do this is to say, "The *company* needs you to do *X*," rather than, "*I* need you to do *X*." The message should be, "There are goals the company needs to achieve. Here's where we are in our metrics. The company is not achieving the performance level it needs to reach. If you work on these areas, you will be more successful, your group will be more successful, and the company will be more successful."

WHAT'S IN IT FOR ME?

This brings us to an important point. If you want to really change an organization, you will need to ask a lot from your people. After a long day of working hard for you, striving to reach the cadence you're setting, they will often be physically and/or mentally exhausted. When they go home and look in the mirror, at some point they're going to say, "I'm working so hard, I'm running myself ragged. Why am I doing this? What's in it for me?"

Speaking for myself as a business owner, I always try to make sure I can answer that question for every person at every level of the company—from senior managers to first-line supervisors to direct operators to janitorial workers. I need be able to say: *here's* what's in it for you.

There may be many answers to the question, "What's in it for me?" For some workers, it might be a sense of camaraderie and teamwork. For others, it might be the possibility of advancement in the company. For a lot of folks, obviously, it's money—in the form of raises and bonuses. All of these things are important and must be addressed. But they're only short-term motivators. In my experience, money doesn't *keep* people motivated. If it did, you wouldn't see $15 million-a-year quarterbacks complaining about how miserable they are in their thankless jobs.

The things that *really* reward people are higher on the spectrum of human needs. I believe people need to (1) feel a sense of achievement, (2) feel acknowledged and valued, and (3) believe they are part of something meaningful.

The third of these points flows from the vision you set for the company. It needs to inspire people. If your vision is simply, "Be profitable this year," don't be surprised if your people lack a heroic sense of purpose. But if your vision is, "We're going to teach the world how to be a green plastics company," or, "We're going to be the most successful company our industry has ever seen," people can rally behind the vision and feel as if they're part of something important. Keep communicating the vision and reminding people of their role in it.

As for the first two points—acknowledgment and a sense of achievement—your job as a leader is to find ways to provide these. One way I came up with to do a little of both for my direct operators is something I call an earned-hour competition. I run four manufacturing shifts—A, B, C, and D—each day, 24–7. As part of our metrics system, we rate the labor efficiency of every shift, and at the end of each month, we give an award to the shift that has had the most efficient shift. I write a personal thank-you letter to that shift, addressed to each individual, and I walk that letter out to each of them, along with a $50 bill. Not a check, but cash, so they can do whatever they want with it. I hand it to the employee, and I say, "This is for you. I appreciate the work you're doing. You're important to this company, and you make a difference. Thank you." That person gets one-on-one recognition from the highest level of the company, a sense of competitive achievement, and also a $50 bill in their pocket.

That's just one small example. Your management and sales teams will need different approaches, obviously. The point is that you should be ready, at all times, to give everyone in the company a compelling answer to the question, "What's in it for me?"

IT'S ALL ABOUT TRUST

Ultimately, everything I've been talking about here comes down to one thing: trust. Real change depends on trust. And trust takes time to build. That's why organizational change always takes time and can't be rushed or dictated. Trust, like respect, must be earned. And that occurs only over time—but it can be lost in a minute.

Trust is absolutely essential. Trust—between coworkers, between managers, between labor and management, between customer and supplier—is the heart and soul of any great organization. And the number one dysfunction in any team is *lack* of trust. When you're in any sort of relationship, at work or at home or in the marketplace, and the other party says, "I don't trust you," that's huge. Your relationship is pretty much over at that point.

You can't directly control whether people trust you or not. You can only behave in a trustworthy manner at all times and *allow* trust to build. People lose trust when they feel you're not being forthright and communicating openly with them. They lose trust when you fail to keep your word or when you promise levels of achievement you can't deliver. They lose trust when you miss your deadlines, fail to follow through on initiatives, or behave in ways that are incongruous with your words. When you lose trust, your power as a change agent becomes almost nil.

As trust in you starts to *grow*, however, the momentum for change starts to shift in your direction. People climb aboard your bandwagon. Relationships strengthen. Loyalty builds. And change starts to become inevitable rather than impossible.

CHAPTER 4

HOPE IS NOT A PLAN

I've made the point several times that business is, first and foremost, a *human* enterprise. But I've also talked about the importance of metrics and data and how essential these elements are to running a growing business. You might be wondering how these two worlds can possibly come together in a productive way—the messy world of *Homo sapiens* and the seemingly sterile world of numbers and quantifiable processes. Isn't relying on metrics to run your business somehow antithetical to running a people-first business? Isn't it a bit "inhuman"?

The short answer is no. The long answer is … well, what this chapter is all about. Understanding the relationship between the realm of quantifiable, measurable processes and the world of human beings is critical to business success.

People and processes are the twin drivers of any growing, successful company. Once you begin to see how the two come together in a dynamic way, you can start to build a business with limitless potential. However, if you only focus on only one—or neither—of these drivers, you'll be running a business based on hope. And hope is not a plan.

In this chapter we're going to look at the importance of processes in the day-to-day running of a business. And we'll also examine some ways to get the most from the people who are running those processes.

WHAT I LEARNED AT GM AND ENGINEERING SCHOOL

I've always been fascinated by predictable, orderly processes. That might sound boring, but it's actually incredibly liberating. When you develop a solid process for achieving results, you can then follow that process over and over again while freeing up your creativity for other things.

For me, my fascination with processes grew out of my work ethic. I've always had a strong work ethic, which, as I told you, I learned from my mother. I watched her go out into the world and work three jobs in order to afford good things for her family. She would set her mind on a goal, and she'd buckle down and work for it. It wasn't the work itself I admired—I don't have any particular affinity for hard labor—it was the discipline and the results. *I* wanted some of those results too. So the first goal I set for myself was to buy my own bicycle.

To achieve that goal, I started cutting neighbors' lawns. I told you earlier, I wasn't a born entrepreneur. That's true. I never came up with a brilliant idea for turning lemonade stands into the next Jamba Juice, but I did know how to work and save. By my early teens, I was mowing two dozen lawns a week, plus doing other odd jobs. And saving a trunk load of money. Not only did I buy that bicycle, but also when I was eighteen, I walked into a car dealership and bought a brand-new car with cash. I did it by following a plan, a process.

I knew what kind of car I wanted, and I knew how many dollars I needed to save each week to get it. And I followed the plan. Buying that car gave me a tremendous feeling of success. How many kids buy a brand-new car with (legally earned) cash at age eighteen?

That success showed me the benefits of sticking to a process. It also prepared me mentally for working at General Motors, the process capital of the world. After high school, I got a full-time job at GM, working fifty-five hours a week while I went to engineering college nights. I learned two powerful lessons at GM, one positive and one negative, which would form the backbone of my thinking about processes and people.

LESSON 1—THE POSITIVE

The first of these lessons was that when enormously complex projects are broken down into small pieces, they become doable.

Growing up, as I've said, I was in love with cars—driving them, wrenching on them, waxing them. My whole family was; 10W-40 ran in our veins. Oddly enough, though, when I started at GM, I still had no idea how cars were actually designed and put together. It was at GM where I learned that the making of a highly complex car is broken down by teams. Each team works on one section. That section is then broken down into individual pieces, with personnel assigned to each part. Everyone is on a timing plan dictating when their part needs to be finished. And when the build date arrives, everything comes together in a way that seems almost magical. All because everyone followed their individual processes, tied to an overall process.

What I learned through my combined experience at GM and engineering school was that *everything* in life is a process. And if you pay careful enough attention, you can identify the steps in

If you want achievable results that you can replicate in a predictable way, you need a process. And the more specific and less subjective that process is, the better.

that process and refine them. If you develop a good process, you can articulate it to others. And if you *follow* that process, then what comes out the other end is the result you're looking for. You can then use that process, again and again, to achieve the same results.

That may sound simplistic and self-evident, but I meet people in business all the time who don't seem to understand that. *If you want achievable results that you can replicate in a predictable way, you need a process. And the more specific and less subjective that process is, the better.*

To develop and implement a process requires discipline, however. Interestingly, discipline is also a topic that many businesspeople misunderstand …

LESSON 2—THE NEGATIVE

When I worked at GM, the company had an extremely regimented work environment. You punched in at 7:00 a.m., you marched straight to your drafting board, and you put your head down and went to work. You had a supervisor and a manager in your area who looked over the drafting boards every minute of the day. You ate lunch from 11:45 a.m. to 12:30 p.m., and if you missed that window, you didn't eat. There was no chitchat around the coffee maker. The drafting room was as quiet as a funeral hall. It was very old world, almost like a workhouse in a Dickens novel.

There was no talking or collaboration between peers. The whole communication structure was completely top down. It relied entirely on an external, military type of discipline—the bosses cracked a whip, and the workers responded.

I didn't love the atmosphere at GM—in fact, I found it uncomfortable and, yes, dehumanizing—but I accepted it. I had nothing to compare it to; I thought this was how companies worked.

One day I had an experience that woke me up. It was a small thing, but it affected me deeply. I was eighteen years old, walking down a hallway at GM, and the top manager of the program, a guy about sixty, was walking toward me. I said, "Good

I still remember that incident vividly. It was a turning point for me. I decided in that moment that if I were ever to be put in charge of a work environment, I would run it very differently.

morning." He put his head down and completely ignored me. It took every bone in my body not to stop, turn around, and say, "Excuse me, I said good morning to you, and I would appreciate a response."

I still remember that incident vividly. It was a turning point for me. I decided in that moment that if I were ever to be put in charge of a work environment, I would run it very differently. I would encourage collaboration and camaraderie. I would welcome smiling faces and the sound of conversation. I would not treat people like pieces of machinery.

I knew discipline was important, but I knew there had to be a better way to achieve it.

PROCESS IS KING

Today I do my best to create an open, collaborative, enjoyable atmosphere in which everyone is valued for their humanity and their talents. We don't punch in at MMI, and no one watches the clock.

People collaborate with their peers, not only in their own departments but in other departments as well. There is mutual respect, interconnectedness, and teamwork.

And yet we run a very disciplined workplace. If we didn't, there is no way we could be growing as steadily and successfully as we are.

So how did I reconcile the two? How is it possible to create an open, pleasant, and collaborative atmosphere while also achieving unprecedented levels of discipline?

The answer is process. Process creates its own discipline. Being aware of the goals you need to attain as an employee, having a clearly defined process for attaining them, and receiving objective, real-time feedback on how you are performing relative to those goals are the key. A process-driven system allows *internal* discipline to blossom, rather than *external* discipline.

Internal discipline is *self*-discipline, and it is vastly more pleasant than external discipline. Internal discipline means *you* accept adult responsibility for meeting your goals, without the need for a disciplinarian cracking the whip. You manage your own work process and your own work habits. In a system of internal discipline, everyone accomplishes more while also enjoying a work atmosphere that is relaxed, collaborative, and free of tension.

External discipline:

- requires a drill sergeant to keep the troops in line

- creates tension between the boss and the workers

- engenders resentment in workers

- treats people like children

- fails to encourage growth

- is militaristic and unpleasant

- breaks down whenever the whip isn't being cracked

- is based on a top-down structure

Internal discipline:

- transfers responsibility to the individual

- allows people to own their tasks and goals

- permits people to solve problems their own way

- removes most interpersonal tensions from the workplace

- treats people like adults

- strongly encourages personal/professional growth

- creates buy-in from team members

- encourages teamwork and collaboration

- produces less employee turnover and burnout

The secret to creating internal discipline is to make process king. Establish a process, continually refine that process, give everyone objective feedback on their performance (via live metrics), and make sure there are checks and balances along the way.

The process itself is impersonal. The metrics that measure people's progress are impersonal. However, the way people rise to meet their individual goals is *very* personal. The way they work together to mutually support one another is very personal. And the feeling of achievement they receive when a goal is met as a result of everyone doing their part is very personal.

When you take the personal out of the system, you give it back to the individual.

PAIRING PEOPLE WITH PROCESS

As I described in chapter 2, creating a productive process starts with having clear and specific goals for the company. These are then broken down into quantifiable goals for each department, group, and individual. Measurables are then created, and the measurables are tracked in an open, observable way that everyone can see. Everyone knows exactly what they need to achieve on an hourly, shift-by-shift, daily, weekly, monthly, quarterly, and annual basis. This allows everyone to set the proper cadence for getting the job done.

If everyone is clear about what they need to be achieving, and the system is clear about providing feedback, there is no need for external discipline of the type I labored under at GM. Yes, you still need leaders who model the right cadence and energy level, but you don't need people barking orders and intimidating their direct reports. When people are given clear information about what they need to accomplish, why it is important, and how they are progressing, they can accept personal responsibility for staying on track.

Of course, this all starts by hiring the right people—quality individuals who are *capable* of internal discipline. And you also have to put the right people in the right places. **Job descriptions** and **performance reviews** are two crucial tools you can use for integrating the right people with your processes and fostering a sense of internal discipline.

JOB DESCRIPTIONS

It has been my observation that in many workplaces, people have a tendency not to "stay in their swim lane." They don't know where their work starts and where it ends. They don't understand their role in the process. They spend a lot of time looking at others' work areas and blaming someone else for any problems that exist. It is critical, therefore, to make sure everyone has a thorough job description that clearly defines where their role starts and stops.

At MMI, everyone who joins the company gets a letter from me on day one welcoming them to our team. They also receive a detailed job description that explains all their roles and responsibilities. They are given a set of ninety-day goals and are told exactly what's expected of them. They receive a full training plan, outlined by week, for the first eight weeks they're employed with us. They are told precisely what they need to be learning every week and what they need to be trained in, and until that training plan is signed off 100 percent and placed in their employee folder, they are not considered to have been fully trained.

Once their training is complete and they have met their ninety-day goals, they are given annual goals to work toward, so they know exactly what they're supposed to do and how to do it.

We then tell our new hires, in effect, "You now have the authority and autonomy to do your job. We're not going to be standing over your shoulder every day. We're not your babysitter. You know your roles and responsibilities. You know where your job starts and where it stops, and you know what your goals are. So go work on them every day." And that pretty much sums up our attitudes and expectations. It's all about owning your part in the process.

PERFORMANCE REVIEWS

Our performance reviews are also directly tied to our process, and we try to take the emotional and personal out of them to the extent possible.

Nowadays, 360 reviews are all the rage in business. To do a 360 review, you gather feedback from everyone in the employee's 360-

degree sphere—their subordinates, their peers, their supervisors. The idea is to give the employee a complete picture of how he/she is regarded in the company. I don't care for 360 reviews. They are personal and subjective, and their recipients tend to focus only on the negative remarks. As soon as they receive their report, they immediately want to figure out, "Who said that about me?"

Our review process is quite different. It is seamlessly integrated with where the company is heading and what its goals are. I'll give you a brief, digested description of how it works.

It all starts with where the company itself is heading. Every year I meet offsite in July with my operations, finance, and sales teams. One of our main agenda items is to start planning our goals for the following year.

Following this meeting, I ask each department to start putting together a draft of their plan for next year, and I give them until September to submit it to me. First, the operations plan is put behind the sales plan, and then the costs are put behind that, and pretty soon I have my first draft of an annual operating plan (AOP). Based on that early draft, I start to put together *my* overall plan as to what the company's goals should be for the next year.

I limit myself to ten bullet points or fewer. I take these top ten goals and write the name of each department below them—sales, engineering, manufacturing, finance, IT, etc. I then ask: "What does each department need to do to help the company achieve these top ten goals?" And then I write bullet points for each department—the goals it will need to achieve to support the company in reaching *its* goals. Around the second week of October, I give this document to my management team. They have until the end of October to add their comments. I then do a final review and publish a document containing all the new departmental goals on November 1.

Then, and only then, do I turn the managers loose to write their employees' performance reviews. As they do this, they simultaneously create SMART (specific, measurable, achievable, relevant, time-bound) goals for each employee for the upcoming year. These SMART goals are designed to support the department's goals, which in turn support the company's goals.

Those reviews are turned in to HR on December 1. We then sit down as a team and look at the SMART goals for *every single person in the company*, and we ask whether these goals align realistically with the department's goals and the company's goals for the new year. If they don't, we make adjustments.

Finally, in the second and third weeks of December, the manager hands the performance review to each employee. The review basically says, "Here's how you performed as an individual relative to last year's SMART goals. Here are your new SMART goals for next year. Here's how those goals align with the goals for the department and the company. Here are the areas you need to work on to be ready to start hitting your goals as of January 2 of next year."

So everyone receives their review right before the holiday. People then have time to reflect and prepare for the new year. And when we start production up again after the holiday, each person knows exactly what the new metrics are, why we established them, and what he or she needs to do to hit their targets. From day one of the new year, we're all rowing in the same direction, and everyone is aligned with one another. No secrets, no surprises.

The performance review thus becomes an integral and essential aspect of how the company reaches its goals. It's not an abstract, subjective thing with dubious value. It is specific, metrics driven, and goal driven, and it puts the ball in the employee's court, where it belongs.

I believe the reason the state of Michigan just gave us the Strategically Focused Award is that every process we design in our company is tied directly to our overall strategy, and every employee is tied directly to the process by quantifiable expectations, roles, and metrics.

BENCHMARKING—THE HEART OF METRICS

Good metrics are absolutely essential to running a successful, growing company. Metrics are the glue that binds your people to your processes. If you're not using metrics, you're running on hope, not a plan. If you want to be an *outstanding* company, however, you also need to incorporate *benchmarking* into the metrics you use in your business. Benchmarking, as you probably know, is the practice of comparing your company's processes, products, and outputs to those of the best companies in your industry.

I continually tell our people our aim is not to be average. Our aim is to be best in class. We want to be the standard by which other companies measure themselves. And the way to get there is not by hoping and trying; it's by learning what the best in the business are doing—in specific, measurable terms—and holding ourselves to meeting or exceeding their standards.

As a leader, you *must* look at benchmarks for your industry and similar industries. You must find experts in your industry who can define best practices for you. And you must always compare your business processes and practices to those in the top quartile of your sector.

In my case, as the leader of MMI, benchmarking was the concept that led me to my love affair with metrics, and so, for me, metrics and benchmarking have always gone hand in hand.

How it all started was this: When I joined MMI, we were a $10 million-a-year company. The products we made were relatively small and simple. But we wanted to grow the company. And we were starting to work on more complex products. As we began to move in that direction, we quickly recognized that the penalties associated with making these more complex products were significant. In other words, if we messed up, our mess-ups would be costlier than ever, in a number of ways.

It happened that around this same time, the automotive industry was also becoming more serious about the quality certifications its suppliers needed to meet. These new standards required suppliers to have a policy, a procedure, and a work instruction in place for everything that occurred in the company—from the way you design, develop, and manufacture parts to the way you invoice, collect money, and manage your whole business.

This combination of two pressures made us sit up and say, "Hey, we need more discipline. Fast. We need to improve our overall financial performance and run a tighter ship, operations-wise." And that was when we really started to get smart about what we were doing. We reached out to some consultants in our manufacturing sector and said, "What are some benchmarks we should be looking at for managing our business better?" And Plante Moran, a business consultancy firm, stepped forward with some answers for us. They said, "We have a good set of metrics for your industry, and here they are."

For the first time, we were able to look at our performance against the best in the business. And the news wasn't good; we weren't in the top quartile. And for one main reason: we'd never really measured how we were doing. We had never quantified things like our on-time deliveries, our costs to produce, our purchase price variances, and dozens of other factors. But now, seeing how the best-in-class companies were performing in these areas gave us a wealth of information we could use to improve our business.

That was when we discovered that we really needed a set of corporate metrics to track all the factors important to our business and to hold ourselves to a new, higher standard. So we put software in place to track all that stuff, and we've never looked back. At first we were tracking too many metrics—pages and pages of them for each department. But what we found over time was that we could whittle those metrics down to a core set that could fit on one piece of paper. The real essentials. And if any of *those* metrics were off, we could drill deeper using more refined metrics to find out why we weren't performing to benchmark status.

Today, because we have benchmarks baked into our metrics, and those metrics are on display for all to see, we know, every hour of every day, what we need to be doing to be best in class.

PUTTING THE HUMAN BACK IN HUMAN CAPITAL

Of course, all the metrics and benchmarks in the world mean nothing without the people who execute them; metrics are just numbers on a computer screen. *People* are the means by which abstract metrics become tangible products and achievements. And you must treat your people as if they are your most important asset. If you're going to ask folks to strive to be best in class, day in and day out, you need to give back to them as well. The exchange of value has to be a two-way street.

Some of what you give your employees can be in the form of compensation, bonuses, and benefits. But you also need to offer things like flexible work hours and on-site workout facilities: things that can improve people's quality of life and let them create a healthy work/life balance. And of course, you must make the work atmosphere pleasant, warm, collaborative, and comfortable. If you want to attract the best in class, you must provide an attractive workplace. A lot of that comes down to the intangibles—respect, appreciation, autonomy, and a meaningful use of people's talent.

Though it might seem, at first glance, that a metrics-driven work environment can strip the human element away, I hope I have shown how the opposite can be true. When you have objective metrics leading the cadence, you take much of the personal tension out of the atmosphere. Instead of employees feeling resentful about breaking their backs for Ted the Tyrant, they feel as if they're working *together* as a team of adults to reach the *company's* goals. There's less of a sense of bosses wielding authority over underlings, less of a sense of "us versus them" between employees and managers—which results in a more respectful, congenial atmosphere overall, and a more positive attitude toward the company leadership.

And when you're liked and respected as a leader, instead of hated and resented, you can do simple things for your employees that go a long way. Simply walking out onto the floor and giving someone a heartfelt thank-you, for example, can mean a lot. And there are two important practices I always try to make room for: reflection and recognition.

Every now and then, we'll "stop the presses" to reflect on where we've been as a company and for me to show appreciation to the people who've helped us succeed. The day before I wrote this section, in fact, we had such a day. I shut down production and called everyone together. I began by telling a little story. "You all might think I'm a work machine," I said to the group, "because of the hours I keep. But every Saturday I take a break. Laura and I go to a little taco joint we love, and we have an afternoon of reflection. We talk about the things we accomplished that week and the struggles we faced. It's important for all of us to do the same thing as a company. And that's why today we're going to have a day of reflection—a little celebration for the end of the first quarter."

And then I presented the "feast"—tacos from my favorite taco place, catered in for the whole company. As we enjoyed our food, I reflected back on all the progress we had been making. "We're up 53 percent over last year," I said. "That's fantastic. We look different. We feel different. Our quality is better. Our delivery is better. And our customers recognize that." I proceeded to thank the teams and the individuals who had made such progress possible.

My emotions came out that day, and I shed a tear or two. I later heard back from several people that the team, as a whole, had been moved and motivated by the event. The reason was not that I'm a brilliant speaker, but that everyone in the company authentically owned a piece of the company's success. They'd all been given the authority to do their jobs, and they'd all found the discipline within themselves to do those jobs to a high standard, and so now our company's win felt personal to each of them. Do you see how that works?

It's only when people understand the role they play in the company's success, accept individual responsibility for that role, and are given the tools, processes, and support they need to perform that role with excellence that a great business culture can arise ...

CHAPTER 5

A CULTURE OF COMMUNICATION AND COLLABORATION

As a leader who wants to *be* the best in class and also *attract* the best in class to work at my company, there are two stark realities I must confront on a daily basis. One of these is that when I look at my competition, I see that everyone in my industry provides essentially the same products and services as I do. We all use the same basic equipment, we all buy the same plastic pellets, we all follow the same code guidelines. I know that if I want to surpass my competition, I must have a differentiator.

The other stark reality I face is that good employees are hard to find these days. As I write this chapter, we are looking at a below 3 percent unemployment rate. That means when it comes to looking for talent, it's a seller's market out there. People have a *choice* as to where they work. They don't need me; I need them. If I want to attract the best and brightest, again I must have a differentiator.

If I want to attract the best and brightest, again I must have a differentiator. In both cases, my differentiator is the same. It is our culture.

In both cases, my differentiator is the same. It is our culture.

A company's culture is the invisible code of behavior that guides the actions, words, and attitudes of its workforce. If your people are your company's "hardware," then your culture is your company's "software." Culture can't be observed directly, but it can be seen, heard, felt, and experienced through …

- the energy level and the cadence of the work

- the expressions on people's faces and the body language they use

- the pride people take in their work

- the cleanliness and organization of people's work spaces

- the way people dress and groom

- the support employees give to one another

- the openness with which people communicate

- the willingness of employees to go the extra mile

- the sense of teamwork, camaraderie, and shared goals

- the code of ethics by which people operate

… and a hundred other ways.

Culture is bigger than any individual. Culture exists before any particular person joins the company, and it endures after any person leaves. Culture pulls employees into its web, shaping their attitudes and behaviors. A great culture energizes and supports its people. A poor culture does the opposite: it drains them and turns them into disengaged zombies.

Why is culture so important? Well, if you want to achieve success in business, here's a humbling fact: you cannot do it alone. One person, no matter how committed, can only do so much. And the more people you have working for you, the harder it becomes to play the Lone Ranger. If you're going to grow your business, you need to scale it up. And that requires a solid, dependable, trustworthy team. The only way to build such a team is to create a great culture.

In my book, that means your culture must be one of communication and collaboration.

COMMUNICATION

The single greatest factor that shapes the culture of a company is the type of communication that is practiced, consciously and unconsciously, by the company's leadership—on a daily and hourly basis.

HALLMARKS OF GREAT COMMUNICATION

In dynamic company cultures, communication has several key characteristics:

COLLABORATIVE STYLE

A collaborative style of communication is one of the hallmarks of a vibrant culture. In stale, hierarchical cultures, leaders use a top-down, one-way form of communication: I speak, you listen. What this tells the listener is, "Your role is to be seen, not heard. Your input is neither required nor desired." Collaborative cultures, by contrast, use a two-way style of communication, one that actively involves the other party or parties in the process. It's not a monologue; it's a dialogue.

In collaborative communication, everyone matters, and everyone's input is valued. There is open-endedness in the process. The final outcome of any communication is not cast in stone until everyone's input has been collected. Solutions that benefit everyone, not just one party, are sought. In collaborative communication, the aim is to find a common goal that everyone can rally behind, with all parties feeling as if they have played some part in the decision process.

Gathering feedback, therefore, is an essential part of collaborative communication. This might be as simple as stopping and asking the other party what they think, or—in the case of company-wide communications—it might entail asking for people's written feedback and/or holding a meeting in which employees' concerns are heard before a final policy is decided on.

Acknowledgment is another huge part of collaborative communication. You must let the other party know that their input was heard, valued, and taken into consideration.

Of course, in the end, companies are not democracies. Ultimately, the leadership must make the key decisions, but these decisions are always better informed if input is first sought from those who will be affected by the decision. And everyone ends up feeling better about a decision when they believe they played a part in it.

UNDERSTANDING PRECEDES "BEING UNDERSTOOD"

As I've said before, I'm a big believer in Stephen Covey's prescription: "If you want to be understood, seek first to understand." Translation: before you even *think* about what you want to say to someone, listen to them and try to understand them.

Listening is one of the least used but most powerful tools in business today. I recently spoke to someone who majored in communications in college. He told me that in his four years of education on subjects such as presentation skills, business writing, and speech-making, he received exactly one hour of training on listening skills. One hour! And this was in a communication school. Yet listening produces better results than all the speaking techniques in the world.

Listening means more than quietly waiting for the other person to shut up so you can make your next brilliant point. Listening means making the space internally to *really take in* what another person is saying. It means setting aside your personal agenda and being completely open to someone else's thoughts and ideas. It means being genuinely interested in that human being, at least for the few minutes you are spending with them.

Nothing makes a person feel more valued and important than having another person truly listen to them. And nothing creates stronger bonds with others than showing them you truly hear and understand what they are saying. Once you have made the effort to understand a person, that person becomes infinitely more receptive to hearing what *you* have to say.

Think about this. How do you feel when you walk in the door of a shop and the salesperson instantly pounces on you, trying to sell you products, without even knowing your needs and interests? You're put off, right? But when that person strikes up a conversation with you and gets to know you first, finds out about your needs and preferences, and *then* offers you solutions based on your real needs, you have a completely different experience.

All communications work on the same principle. The correct attitude going into a conversation should not be, "I am going to convince you of my point of view." It should be, "I am going to find out what *you* think and feel." Becoming a better listener—and training your whole leadership team to do the same—is one of the most powerful things you can do to create a vibrant culture.

REGULAR AND CONTINUOUS

If you want a great culture, good communication must be the *daily heartbeat* of your company, not just an occasional event. The more frequently you communicate, and the more *ways* in which you communicate, the better. Communicate about the big things and the small things. All the time.

One of the lamest ideas many leaders cling to is that one-time communication works. The top company leader "parachutes in" for a special meeting, spends a few hours delivering his message about how things need to change, and then flies off, thinking he has made a difference. Such messages are quickly forgotten. In order for a message to take, it must be repeated and reinforced over and over again, in countless ways, over a long period of time.

Regular and continuous communication is the key. When you fail to do this, people start to think you have something to hide. You lose people's trust, and you also lose control of the narrative—people start to make up stories to fill in the blanks you're not filling in. You lose people's confidence as well. They don't know where you're going with a particular project or with the company itself, and so they quickly lose sight of how they fit in.

One of the ways we ensure regular and continuous communication at MMI is by distributing a very detailed production report that spells out, in black and while, exactly how efficiently each shift performed—using a number of key variables. We don't wait till a week, a month, or a quarter has passed to tell people where things stand with their teams. We make it a daily thing.

When you communicate constantly—about the big things and the small things—you build a basis of trust and confidence, and people will listen to you when you need them the most.

BUILT ON POSITIVE REINFORCEMENT

An essential element of effective communication is positivity. You must constantly provide positive reinforcement for whatever your team members are working on. That means "catching people doing right" and giving them praise and feedback for their efforts. I suggest spending 80 percent of your time focusing on people's strengths, and building on these, and only 20 percent of your time correcting their flaws and weaknesses. Keep the focus positive.

Look for ways to call out achievement. Just the other day, for example, I announced to the team that we had received our first purchase order from Daimler Trucks—an account we'd been coveting for years. The main credit for that win belonged to the salesperson, Dave, who'd been working his butt off for three years, trying to break down barriers and meet the qualifications needed to get into Daimler. So we stopped production to recognize his efforts.

Now at MMI, each time we add a new customer, we print their company logo in a three- or four-foot size, mount it on foam backing, and post it in our manufacturing plant, so our employees can see who they're making products for. This time I had an extra one of these signs made for Dave with the Daimler logo on it. I brought Dave out in front of the company and said, "I'm giving you this logo because your dedication and hard work in breaking down those barriers are examples to us all." Dave had gone out on a limb to win this account, and we wanted to say, "Well done!" from the entire organization.

Nothing creates a healthy culture more powerfully than openness and honesty. Nothing.

Your style of communication as a leadership team must be one of supporting people in taking risks, not trying to assign blame. In a blame-based culture, people become ultracautious. They're afraid of getting their heads blown off if they make a mistake, so they retreat into their foxholes and try to avoid being noticed. However, if they receive constant positive reinforcement and support, they are much more willing to take chances and be innovative.

People will not go out on a limb and innovate if they feel their job is in jeopardy or they're going to be punished or yelled at as a result of taking a chance. You must make them feel safe.

Remember, people are your greatest asset. So communicate as if that were so.

OPEN AND HONEST

Finally, communication must be open and honest. About both the good and the bad.

It's easy to be open and honest about the good things; it's harder when it comes to the negative and difficult things. All of us seek to avoid conflict, so we often fail to communicate about things we consider problematic or troubling.

Ultimately, though, people would rather hear bad news directly and honestly than learn about it through the grapevine. When people are blindsided by bad news—such as layoffs or changes to their health insurance plans—they become angry, suspicious, and defensive. Conversely, when they see that you're willing to be honest with them regarding both good news and bad news, they begin to trust you as a communicator. And as a person.

This applies to giving feedback about employees' job performance. Though it is important, as I said above, to keep your focus positive, it is also essential that you be open and honest with people when they fall below your expectations. Such communication should be handled tactfully and constructively, in a private setting, but it also must be clear and direct.

Nothing creates a healthy culture more powerfully than openness and honesty. Nothing.

THE REWARDS OF GREAT COMMUNICATION

If you communicate according to the above guidelines, you will see transformative effects in your culture—effects that will flow directly to your bottom line. For example …

AN INCREASE IN TRUST, CONFIDENCE, AND COMFORT

When your communications are regular, open, honest, and listening based, your team begins to trust you and develop confidence in you. Their *comfort* level with you also increases. They get to know you and accept you as a human being. The importance of this cannot be overstated. Experience has repeatedly shown me that customers buy from salespeople they feel comfortable with, and employers hire people they feel comfortable with. The same principle holds true within the workplace.

GREATER LOYALTY

When people like you and feel comfortable with you, they become loyal to you. They are likely to stay at the company much longer and to view the company as family. This longevity leads to a more experienced and knowledgeable workforce, which leads to better products, increased customer trust, and a stronger value proposition for the company. It also leads to less turnover, which greatly reduces your hiring and training costs.

BETTER INFORMATION-SHARING

When people trust and accept you, they are much more likely to share vital information with you. They confide in you about problematic issues they see in the production process. They tell you things they would otherwise keep to themselves. I've had this happen numerous times. I'm walking the floor of the plant, and an employee takes me aside and says, "Hey, Doug, I want to show you something." And suddenly I learn about a safety issue or a process breakdown I was unaware of. Conversely, when trust and acceptance are absent, people have no desire to put themselves at risk by opening their mouths.

ENGAGEMENT AND A WINNING ATTITUDE

When you regularly communicate about where the company is headed and the key role people play in the process, everyone feels important. They realize that what they do matters. Because of that, they feel engaged.

People naturally want to be a part of a winning team. There's no better feeling—in business, sports, or any other field—than winning. Winning is contagious. Losing is contagious as well. It leads to toxic attitudes and a culture of finger-pointing and blaming.

A MORE ATTRACTIVE WORKPLACE

The benefits you gain from good communications translate directly into a more vital, committed, and energetic workplace. That kind of workplace is attractive to outsiders. When people come to your physical plant, they can feel the vibrancy of your culture, and they want to be a part of it. This means you can attract best-in-class talent, which further contributes to a culture of excellence and winning. You also attract customers. When customers get a taste of your positive culture, they want to do business with you. They trust you because they believe excellence is important to you. They want to tap into your culture and make it part of theirs.

WAYS OF COMMUNICATING

Communication includes the words you say and write, obviously, but it entails much more ...

DIRECT COMMUNICATIONS

These are the ways you communicate directly with your team members. They include one-on-one meetings and company gatherings. They also include letters to employees, emails, videos, posters, podcasts, PowerPoints, and speeches. As a rule, the more varied ways you can use to communicate your message the better. Some employees are visual learners; they only remember what they see and read. Others are audio learners. So try to hit people in a variety of ways. And repeatedly. A fact about human cognition is that the more times we see/hear a message, the more likely we are to accept it as true. If I have a critical piece of information I need to share with employees, I will communicate about it verbally, but I'll also put it in a letter in their paycheck envelope—so I'm certain they will *see* it too.

PERSON-TO-PERSON EXCHANGES

Communication doesn't need to be complicated to be effective. Some of the most important communications are the simple, heartfelt *good morning* and *how are you* type greetings. Remembering that an employee's kid plays Little League or that his wife is expecting a baby and asking the person about those things keeps the two of you connected on a human level. Reinforcing that personal connection is one of the most important functions of communication.

"WALKING THE TALK"

A powerful way to communicate the values of the company is by "walking the talk." Exude the kind of energy you expect from your team. Smile. Be willing to roll up your sleeves to help solve a problem or to work late when an important project needs to be kept on track.

If there's a problem on the late shift, be willing to come in at midnight and sit with the operators and figure it out. When your team is meeting with an outside customer over a difficult issue and you know it's going to be an unpleasant meeting, go with them to the meeting—not to communicate that you don't trust them, but to say, "I'm not sending you in to get your head chopped off alone. I'm here to give you my support."

The absolute best way to communicate your expectations of others is to embody those expectations in everything *you* say and do. Actions speak louder than words—you heard it here first.

THE "QUALITY WALK"

An important ritual I perform every week at my company is something I call the "quality walk." I simply walk from one end of the plant to the other, taking time to observe what's going on, ask questions, say hello to all of my employees, and give everyone a chance to ask me questions or bring things to my attention. I have no agenda on these walks except to check in with everyone. But the walks typically last for hours as I become engaged with people over a wide variety of topics—a great communication tool.

COLLABORATION

The other vital aspect of a great culture is collaboration. Collaboration, in my definition, means that everyone in the company is working together toward a common goal. Everyone tries to help everyone else do their jobs better so that the company as a whole can improve. And everyone's input is valued.

A collaborative culture is one in which blaming is not tolerated and in which everyone accepts personal responsibility for making processes more efficient, workable, and profitable. There is no attitude of, "That's someone else's problem," because all jobs in the company are seen as interconnected. For example, the engineers know that a sloppy piece of engineering can lead to extra man-hours for the manufacturing team. That can affect the profit margins the finance department is counting on. It can also cause shipping delays, which can mess up the shipping department's schedule as well as the sales team's relationships with its customer.

There is no "someone else" to blame in a collaborative culture. Everything that happens in a company affects everything else, and everyone shares a responsibility to solve any problem that arises. Everyone also shares equally in the triumphs of any department, and of the company as a whole.

Here are a few ways I try to build a collaborative culture.

THE WORLD'S BEST
MANAGEMENT TOOL: THE MIRROR

Whenever someone on my management team says something like, "We'd be doing great if the engineering team would just get its act together," I say something like this: "Everyone, please pick up a mirror. You are looking at the person who is going to solve this problem. The reason this problem is happening is because we, the management team, have failed to hire the right people, train people the right way, put the right processes in place, or establish the right set of checks and balances. So what are *we* going to do about it?"

When some people hear the word *collaborative*, they think it means having less individual responsibility and more reliance on the group. The opposite is actually true. A collaborative culture is *built* on personal responsibility. When everyone has the attitude, "What can *I* do?"—rather than, "Who's to blame for this?"—that's when people are truly ready to work together in a collaborative way.

Personal responsibility must be emphasized in all of your team interactions. For example, here's a typical scenario. You're in a meeting talking about a problem in one of your work processes. Someone proposes a solution, and the inevitable naysayer immediately chimes in with, "That's not gonna work." It's important, as a collaborative leader, to say to these habitual naysayers, "Okay, you don't seem to like the solutions that have been offered. Tell us how *you* would solve the problem." Hand them the mirror, and see what happens.

CROSS-FUNCTIONALITY

One of the most powerful ways to establish a collaborative culture in an organization is to create cross-functional responsibility. By that I mean you make the success of each department dependent on the success of other departments. You also make individual bonuses dependent on similar criteria.

At MMI, no one is allowed to just do their job, hand it off, and walk away with the attitude that it's now someone else's problem. Our philosophy is that all company functions are interconnected, and every decision you make needs to be workable across the whole company, not just for your department or for yourself as an individual. I'll give you a couple of examples.

Sales. In sales, everyone naturally wants to go out and sell a lot of business so they can get their sales numbers up. But sometimes these sales are not "quality" sales. Sometimes they bring in business that increases the company's top line without increasing its bottom line. When the engineering and manufacturing teams try to execute these jobs, they find they can't do them at a decent profit margin. These kinds of jobs are terrible for the company. In other cases, salespeople sometimes sign deals with deadbeat companies from whom the billing department has trouble collecting payments. Again, no good.

That's why, at MMI, salespeople must meet certain criteria beyond their sales numbers in order to receive their commissions. First, each piece of business they bring in must be executable at a >30 percent profit margin, and second, each customer they sign must be financially stable and must actually pay their bills. These criteria force the salespeople to be more communicative and collaborative with other departments when selling new business.

Engineering. Another example is in engineering. Formerly in our company, the engineers would design and develop a new tool and then hand it off to the operations team to manufacture the product and ship it. The engineers would lose responsibility for the tool the moment they handed it off. But what would sometimes happen was that the operations team would have trouble hitting its cost, quality, and efficiency metrics when trying to make products with this new tool. The engineers would blame the operators, but often the problem lay with the engineers themselves. The product and the process they had designed were flawed in some way.

So we started to apply the metrics from the operations side to the engineering side. We said to the engineers, "Your bonus is now attached to how well the operations team performs when working with your tools." Instantly the work environment became more collaborative. Now we had the engineers sitting down with the operators and saying, "What can we do to make your job go more smoothly? What changes can we make?" Collaboration.

I recently sent out letters to all my department heads, explaining that their bonuses would now be tied to the performance of the entire company, as measured by several metrics—such as customer delivery percentages and percentages of scrap (waste) produced. Perhaps you're wondering how departments such as finance and human resources could possibly bear any responsibility for the amount of scrap the manufacturing process produces. Well, think about it: maybe the finance department needs to identify which specific parts are producing the scrap so that the waste problem can be targeted. Maybe the HR department needs to say, "Perhaps our workers are creating waste because we're hiring people with the wrong skills, or we're failing to provide the proper training." See how everything is connected?

In such an interconnected system, the only culture that makes sense is a collaborative one.

AUTONOMY

In order for a collaborative culture to exist, there must be autonomy throughout the organization. When all decisions are made in a top-down fashion, you end up with a military-style culture—as I worked under at GM—not a collaborative one. For this reason, I always give my managers plenty of room to operate. And they give *their* direct reports the same kind of leeway, to the extent possible.

What this collaborative style of management says is, "In order for us to succeed, we *all* need to make managerial contributions. I'm counting on each of you to bring your particular talents and ideas to the table."

When you use collaborative management, you benefit from a wide variety of perspectives. Many heads are better than one. Sometimes the way a front-line worker creatively solves a problem gives you the key for solving an even bigger problem elsewhere in the company. Sometimes the way a particular manager addresses an issue becomes a new procedure for the whole company. These ideas arise only when people have the freedom to make decisions.

As I've said before, I would rather have people take risks and fail than not take risks at all. Risk-taking happens only in a collaborative culture where decision-making is distributed, not centralized.

WHAT A CULTURE OF COMMUNICATION AND COLLABORATION LOOKS LIKE

We've all seen crummy business cultures. The physical plant has a cluttered, disorganized look. Equipment is broken and dirty; there is a sense of neglect. Customers are treated like inconveniences. Managers walk right by problem areas as if they don't see them. People's postures look defeated or defensive. Workers don't speak to one another, and when they do, it's often in anger. The place becomes a ghost town at five o'clock.

By contrast, a great culture (i.e., a culture of communication and collaboration) has a distinctly positive flavor. You can taste it when you walk in the door. People have smiles on their faces, a light in their eyes, and a kick in their steps. Animated conversations occur in the halls. You hear frequent laughter. People take pride in their work areas and are willing to stay late to finish projects. Equipment is clean and functional. There is energy in the air.

But perhaps the surest hallmark of a great culture is this: employees are more interested in *being* good than in *looking* good. In poor cultures, everyone passes the buck, and no one wants to take risks—they are too afraid of looking bad. In great cultures, everyone has a stake in the success of everyone else in the company. So the motivation is always to *actually be* the best, not to just look good in order to avoid being yelled at. When employees adopt a *personal mission to excel*, that's when your company is on track for limitless success.

And that type of personal mission-making happens only when individuals are driven by a sense of passion and purpose.

CHAPTER 6

PASSION PROVIDES PURPOSE

Communication and collaboration form the foundation of a great culture, but if I had to pick one single element that differentiates a truly outstanding culture from a "meh" culture, it would be passion.

By passion, I simply mean excitement, energy, enthusiasm, and a sense of fun. When you have that kind of vibe in your business, it is contagious. People get swept up in it and want to be part of it. In turn, they begin to care about the products they are making and the team they are working with. And that leads to a sense of purpose.

That's how championship teams are built in sports. That's how championship teams are built in business too. Passion leads to purpose leads to a winning mentality.

Passion is the flame that ignites people's energy. It's the fire in people's eyes and bellies. But that flame must be fed, constantly, or else it burns out. Purpose is the fuel that feeds passion's fire on a long-term basis. Purpose is the belief that what I am doing every day *matters*. In a great company, passion and purpose feed each other in a virtuous cycle.

Passion is not an easy quality to generate and sustain. For that reason, many leaders don't even bother trying to create it. But that is huge mistake on their part. I believe there are many things a leader can do to create, encourage, and inspire passion in a company.

IT ALL STARTS WITH YOU

Once again, the mirror is your first tool of choice. In order for passion to spread in a company, it *must* begin with the leadership. Passion is not one of those qualities that can arise from within the rank and file and bubble up to the top. It *must* start at the top.

The leadership—that means *you*—*must* show excitement, energy, and positivity on a daily and an hourly basis. The other members of your leadership team must show these things too. Anyone on your leadership team who does not exude passion for the work they do must be radically retrained or terminated.

Passion is one of the most important qualities a leader can possess. But it can't be faked, not over the long term. That's why it is so vital that you, as the business owner and/or leader, carefully choose the type of business you are going to lead. You can't just pick a business because you think it will make money hand over fist. As I've said before, making money is not enough to sustain and motivate you toward prolonged excellence, nor is it enough to attract and motivate a dedicated team of high-quality employees. You'd better have a deeper, more passionate connection to the products and services you're providing.

Me, I'm a car guy. I've always loved cars and everything about them. I devour news stories about cars and the auto industry. I'm genuinely excited to be in a position where the products and processes my team designs have a real effect on an industry I love. That's what gets my blood pumping. That doesn't mean I never have a low-energy day, but it does mean my energy always replenishes itself—because I'm doing what I love to do.

I remember a guy I used to work with at my previous job. I'll call him Greg. Greg was a nice guy, he really was, but he had absolutely zero interest in the automotive industry. He got his job because his father-in-law owned the company. The rest of us would be sitting around the office chatting, and one of us would say something like, "Hey, did you hear GM just announced they're going to be unveiling the new Corvette in July?" And Greg would say, "I don't care about that. I hate cars," and walk away.

Greg had a right to dislike cars, of course, but why did he choose to work in this business? His lack of passion meant that he brought no good energy to the job and was a constant drain on the enthusiasm of others. He was absolutely incapable of inspiring other employees, because he didn't care about the products we were making. So he was doing both himself and the company a disservice by being in the business.

Whatever business you decide to enter, make sure your passion is real—at least for *some* aspect of the business (besides making money). For example, you might not feel giddily excited about cleaning septic tanks for a living, but you *might* feel passion about performing an important service that makes people feel better about living in their homes. Find your authentic passion for some key aspect of the work, and exude it every day.

Remember this caveat too: we all express passion differently. Not everyone is the fist-pumping, jump-up-and-down type. Some people exhibit passion in other ways—quiet excitement, working extra hard to get things right, dedicating themselves to excellence. Allow everyone in your team, including yourself, to express passion in their own authentic ways.

FINDING THE RIGHT PEOPLE

The next-most important step in creating passion is to choose the right people for your company. Passion can spread through a company only when you have passionate people on your payroll and only when these people are encouraged to form a real connection with one another. When you continually choose the right people, and put them in the right positions, you are able to continue to attract even *more* of the right people to your company.

PERSONALITY FIT

One of the most important hiring considerations is personality. It goes without saying that the candidate for any position must be qualified, first and foremost. They must have the right skills and experiences. But that's just the starting point. An even more important consideration is, "How will this unique human being fit in with the other unique human beings on my team?"

Think about the way a smart baseball manager or football GM chooses a new team member. Of course they look at the player's stats—batting averages, tackles per game, etc.—but stats are only one piece of the puzzle. They also look at a host of other considerations. How will this player get along with other key players on the team? Will there be any personality clashes? What kind of locker-room presence will this player be? How will he respond to our style of coaching and game planning? Is he a jerk? An egomaniac? Is he coachable? Does his personality gel with the brand and values of our team? Does he have talents that will blossom under our style of leadership? Will he thrive in our particular media market? And so on.

You must consider the same types of factors when doing your hiring. First, does the candidate have passion for some aspect of the company's products or mission? If not, they're going to be a dead spot; the passion current won't be able to flow through them. Then you have to think about how they will mesh with other important members of your team. In every company, there are key players who are critical to the culture and to the success of the company. You need to think about these key players when hiring new talent.

Will the candidate be able to communicate effectively with these  ve some interests in common, both career-vorld? For example, do they all have kids at : do they have hobbies in common? Do they r Netflix? Do they come from similar areas? ey can talk about? More importantly, will

personality fit on your teams, everyone's Conversely, when people are surrounded by to, they feel uncomfortable and alienated. :ir ability to do their job, but it will affect inicate and form connections with fellow on't feel loyal to the team, which means they -term employees. So it's crucial to look for ersonality, in interests, in priorities, etc.

But here's another important caveat: you also need to be very careful not to inadvertently exclude people of any gender, race, age, ethnicity, religion, political affiliation, etc. The commonalities you look for should be related to personality more than to a particular cultural background. For example, anyone, of any age, race, or gender, might be interested in children, *American Idol*, the food scene, local sports teams, or physical fitness.

An interesting side note: Our management team and workforce at MMI is extremely diverse in terms of gender, age, race, and ethnicity. To an outsider's eye, it might seem as if we follow some kind of strict quota system to achieve this diversity, but we have never done so. By focusing on inner qualities such as passion, motivation, commitment, self-confidence, team fit, and interests, we have found that the "outer" mix takes care of itself. This approach might not work for every company and every situation, but it has worked for us.

BRING IN YOUR "PASSION TEAM"

One thing I like to do during the hiring process is to bring in some of those key players who exude passion and embody the values we cherish as a company. We invite these people to be part of the interview process. We do this so that they can ask specific questions about the candidate's skills and experiences, but more importantly, so we can see the kind of chemistry that develops between the candidate and the key players. If we notice an increase of energy in the room, hear a few laughs, and see a collective sense of excitement and positivity, there's an excellent chance that candidate will be a good fit.

TWO KEY PERSONALITY TRAITS

Besides passion, enthusiasm, and being a good fit for the team, there are two other personality traits I find essential to creating winning and innovative teams: curiosity and creativity. Both of these traits are the hallmarks of active minds.

Maybe I have a soft spot for curious people because I have always been one myself. I've always been interested in learning the story *behind* things. I want to know the details of how a business works, how a product is developed, how technologies are invented, things like that. That general curiosity has always fueled a desire to learn more.

That was what motivated me to pursue my MBA and law degree after getting my engineering degree. My multifaceted education, together with my experience, has enabled me to put together a business plan that is not only functionally sound but financially sound as well.

When people follow their curiosity, they become more well rounded and are able to see a situation from more than one side. This invariably makes them more valuable employees. An engineer who knows something about the business side of the industry will design products in a more informed way than someone who knows only the math and physics. A person who has actually driven an eighteen-wheeler will design a loading dock more thoughtfully than someone who hasn't. I love to hire curious, well-rounded people.

I love to hire curious, well-rounded people. Curious people tend to be passionate people, and to inspire passion in others.

Curious people tend to be passionate people, and to inspire passion in others.

A trait that often goes hand in hand with curiosity is creativity. When I say creativity, I don't necessarily mean the ability to write a symphony. I mean the desire to make something new and to have some control over the creative process. So a trait I always look for when hiring is a hunger to bring something into the world that has never existed before.

When you can provide people opportunities to learn something they're interested in or to create something new, you can generate great energy and passion in the work environment.

On the other end of the spectrum are those employees who have no interest in anything beyond their immediate job responsibilities. These people tend to have passive minds and personalities. This trait often goes hand in hand with laziness. These folks often do the minimum they need to do to get by. They sit at the back of the room in meetings and try to blend in so they won't have to contribute. They are passion killers. You need to identify them and try to inspire and turn them around. If that doesn't work, you need to let them go.

AGE CONSIDERATIONS

Having a diverse workforce, including people of all ages, is in the best interest of everyone in the company. But there are a few age considerations you might want to keep in the back of your mind as you are recruiting, hiring, and training new people—these factors can affect the "passion potential" of your company.

Speaking very generally, people in their thirties and forties tend to be in their most productive years. They've often started families and are laying foundations for a sound financial future. They still have the energy of youth, but it's now coupled with experience and skill. They are willing to work hard and pay their dues. But they're also looking to advance themselves, so unless you provide them advancement opportunities, you'll have a hard time holding on to these folks. It's great to have a nice core of people in this age range on your staff.

Young adults, known today as millennials, often have great technological and media skills—having been raised with computers and smartphones—as well as optimism and energy, but there is one red flag to be aware of. That is, many millennials have a sense of entitlement that isn't warranted. Perhaps this is because they were raised in an era where every kid earned a participation prize just for showing up, instead of for excelling and winning. But my experience has been that young adults of this generation tend to have an inflated sense of their own value as compared to their actual skills.

Entitlement is *deadly* in a company striving for excellence. Everyone needs to be laser-focused on what they're *contributing*, rather than on what they feel entitled to receive. So when you hire young adults today, you may need to instill in them the idea that there is a concrete pathway to achievement. Rewards are given for actual performance only. Nothing is handed to anyone just for showing up, and nothing substitutes for experience and know-how.

We recently had a situation at MMI that highlighted this point. We had nominated several of our workers to be recognized on an industry-wide platform. Two of our people were chosen, one of whom was an older individual, with over fifteen years of experience, the other of whom was a millennial, with only a couple of years of postschool experience.

After the publicity event occurred, the older, more experienced person was humble and modest, deflected all praise, and didn't want to be singled out. The younger person, however, immediately asked for a meeting with the head of HR and said, in essence, "I've been recognized for being an exceptional person. I think my value is substantially higher than what you're paying me, and I should be paid more money." This younger individual *is* a good employee, mind you, but the mind-set exhibited here is one you should be aware of.

There are dangers at the other end of the age spectrum too. Older workers are extremely valuable because of the rich experience they bring to the table and their finely honed skills, but you need to watch out for people on "retirement watch." These are employees who are only interested in hanging on and doing the minimum required until their retirement. They come to work only because they still need something to keep them busy, but in their minds they have one foot out the door. They, too, can be passion killers.

In an ideal scenario, you can pair older workers with millennials in a way that helps both of them and expands the passion quotient for the whole company. We have a great story at MMI that illustrates this. One of our local school systems has what they call a machines-trade program. A lot of kids who go into this program haven't done very well in school and don't know where they're headed in life. Their prospects aren't super great.

We partnered up with this program and started bringing some of these kids in for summer internships. The internships are twelve weeks long, and if the kids do well, we hire them. So in this one case we brought in a kid called Nick. He was a bit lost at sea and didn't know much about anything. We put him in our tool shop and had him sweeping floors and doing other menial tasks to gain exposure to the trade.

It happens that in our tool shop, we have a seventy-four-year-old German journeyman toolmaker, Manny, who likes to coach and mentor young kids. Manny is highly skilled and disciplined. He comes to work early every day and stays late. He pays attention to detail; that's how he shows his passion. And here's a hint about his character. He's been going through chemotherapy for several years, and he's never missed a day of work. He doesn't take any crap from anybody. Manny took Nick under his wing and started to teach him about the toolmaking trade.

Long story short, Manny basically turned Nick's life around. Before long, Nick became engaged in the toolmaking process. He began showing up early. And over the last three years, he has been like a sponge, soaking up Manny's knowledge. He stands at attention whenever Manny is talking to him. He listens to everything Manny has to say. He has developed a passion and an energy for his work, and now he's making almost double what he did when he started.

He has full health care benefits, vacation time, dental, vision, and a 401(k) plan.

Nick now has a clear career path in front of him, and he can't get enough of machining and tooling. It has become his passion in life, and that passion has provided him with his purpose. Now *he's* the one who fires up all the new interns and cheers them on. Nick's story is an amazing illustration of how passion spreads when you put the right people in the right place.

CREATING A FIT

Choosing the right people to hire is just the first step in creating a vibrant workforce. Once the hire takes place, it's now on you to set the tone and engage each new person so they'll become a vital part of your passionate, purposeful team.

SET THE CADENCE ON DAY ONE, HOUR ONE

The most important thing you can do with a new hire is set the tone and the cadence with them immediately. I mean on day one, hour one, minute one. It's a fact of human nature that people expend only as much energy as they think is required for a given situation. If they think they can get away with giving it only 60 percent, that's where they'll set their effort meter. And once someone's meter is set, it's hard to get them to change it later. So it's critical that you set a brisk cadence and a high level of expectations from the moment people start their first day.

At MMI, we do that by having a human resources person greet each new hire when they walk in the door. They hand the hire a three-ring binder that contains the items I talked about in chapter 4. Page one is a letter from me welcoming them to the MMI family.

Page two is their detailed job description. Page three lists their ninety-day goals. After that, their eight-week training program is laid out in detail.

We show the new person to their desk, which is set up and work ready. Their computer is ready for them to log in and start working. All of their essentials—pens, notepads, paper clips, etc.—are present and waiting. The message we want to send is, "Your MMI career starts *now*."

ESTABLISH A PERSONAL RELATIONSHIP

One of the most important steps I take when bringing any new person aboard is to sit down with them, personally, for a thirty-to-sixty-minute meeting. I talk to them from the heart about the company and where we are today and what we're trying to accomplish. I explain to them the importance of their role and how they can help the business succeed. I make sure they know they are the company's most important asset.

During this meeting they begin to identify with me as a person, and they learn that they can come to me and talk to me anytime. Even more importantly, I get to know *them* as individuals. I ask questions and I listen. Do they have a family? What are their hobbies? What are their interests? Where else have they worked? I try to find a way to identify with every employee, to form a person-to-person connection.

That connection is something I then try to maintain and build upon as time goes on.

MESH PERSONAL INTERESTS
WITH COMPANY GOALS

If you make the effort to get to know the passions and interests of your people, you can try to combine their interests with initiatives that are good for the company. That way, you get a much more engaged employee and the company gains the benefit of that employee's passion.

For example, there are quite a few people at MMI who have a strong passion for health and fitness. The company, for its part, is also interested in having a fit workforce—after all, healthy people take fewer sick days and are more productive. So we have developed a wellness team within the company. One of the team's tasks is to come up with at least one wellness event every month, which the company then sponsors. This could be a 5K run, or a special health presentation, or a day in which we serve trail mix in the break room instead of candy and cookies.

This year we've set aside a space in the plant for an on-site gym for employees. I've tasked the wellness team with designing and building the gym. They have a budget, and they're bringing in contractors and taking bids. They're going out and pricing equipment, often on their own time, and working collaboratively on the design. They own this project, so they've got tons of passion and commitment for it. They're more engaged, and we'll have a healthier staff as a result.

Another way to engage employees is through the community and charity work the company does. You can't expect everyone in a company to be as passionate about the company's mission as you are, but you can often ignite employees' passion and purpose by being a company that contributes to the community and the world. As one example in our company, we're working with the Huron Valley

Humane Society to sponsor a big fund-raising dinner called Paws, Plates, and Community. We're involving not just our employees, but our customers and our vendors—everyone we know. The energy for this project is tremendous, especially among our animal lovers. Work takes on a deeper meaning when you believe your company is a force for good in the world. Loyalty grows as a result of this too.

OFFER INCENTIVES (ANSWER THE QUESTION, "WHAT'S IN IT FOR ME?")

Of course, you must directly incentivize employees as well. You must provide ways to show them gratitude and recognition. We've talked about some ways to do this in previous chapters. Another way we do this at MMI is through a peer-to-peer recognition program we call Pursuit of Excellence. We place stacks of three-copy forms in the break rooms and sign-in areas. Any employee can use these forms to recognize any other employee for exhibiting a positive trait. They might just write, "Thanks, Jim, for staying late to get that shipment out," or "Great job, Emily, offering support to the new guy." They give the white top copy directly to the person being recognized. The yellow copy is posted on a big whiteboard in the middle of the plant for everyone to see. The pink copy goes into a fishbowl in the break room. At the end of the month, we do a random drawing from the fishbowl and award gift cards to the winners.

You also need to allow people to participate in the financial success of the company. We handle that largely through bonuses. At MMI, *everybody* is eligible for a bonus, from the janitor to the senior management. They each have specific goals and criteria they need to meet in order to be eligible. But before those goals are even considered, the company itself has to reach its financial objectives. I tell everyone that whatever you do at MMI, it has to be good for the business first. Then it can be good for the individuals. So we're all pulling for the good of the business, all the time. That's another way we amp up the passion and purpose.

DEVELOP CAREERS

If you want to retain passionate, purposeful employees, you must also keep challenging them and offering them room for growth. Good people aren't content to sit still. And millennials seem to have a two-year timer built into them. After about two years, they start getting restless and thinking about moving on to something new. So you need to be prepped for this eventuality and ready to offer people educational, training, and advancement opportunities. This is a major management challenge.

At MMI the management team always has a running list of employees we call "high pots"—short for high-potential. These are people who show talent and are moving quickly in the company. High pots, as a rule, are always looking for something more to do. They may be advancing their education on the side or talking to headhunters about new opportunities. We sit down with these people and say, "Hey, we noticed you're getting your engineering degree. Talk to us about where you want to go because we like you as an employee and we're a better company with you on board. So we want to make sure we continue to grow your career. I can't know what's on your mind unless you talk to me. So let's continue to have this conversation."

And we try to do that not just once a year but multiple times per year. We sit down with these folks, and we say, "What can we do to help develop you?"

If you'll recall, no one talked to me when I was feeling restless for advancement in my previous job. So I ended up leaving.

Keep the fun and the passion alive. You'll end up with a purpose-driven workforce.

I try not to let the same thing happen to my best and brightest.

* * *

Finally, there is one more thing you can do to keep passion alive in the workplace. And that is simply to *have fun*. Lose the attitude that work needs to be serious in order to get anything accomplished. The fact is that people accomplish more in the long run when they are having a blast and can't believe they're getting paid for what they do. As I was writing this chapter, Magic Johnson resigned as president of the LA Lakers. Why? He wasn't having fun anymore. Fun is important. It's a big reason why we do what we do.

Keep the fun and the passion alive. You'll end up with a purpose-driven workforce.

CHAPTER 7

MAKE IT HAPPEN

B usiness leadership is a skill set that's never complete. In fact, the more I have learned over the years, the more I have discovered I don't know, which has continually forced me to learn even more. To this day, I am a sponge, trying to soak up any new knowledge and skills that I think will help me sharpen my business edge a bit more.

But there are certain key lessons I've taken to heart over the years that really stand out in their power to turbocharge results. It took me decades to learn these "superlessons," but I am sharing them with you in this chapter in the hopes that you will put them to use sooner rather than later. Master these ideas and practices, and your business will be well on its way to becoming the company whose dust trail everyone else is chasing.

If you prefer to *hope* for success, skip this chapter. If you prefer to *make it happen*, read on …

HARNESS THE POWER OF A SCOREBOARD

A scoreboard may be the most powerful tool a business can employ. Imagine trying to win a basketball, football, or baseball championship without being able to see the scoreboard. If none of your players or coaches knew what period it was, how much time was left in the game, what the score was, or where your team stood in the series, how might that affect the way they played the game? How might it change the urgency of their efforts, the type of plays they chose, the strategy they adopted?

A scoreboard provides vital information to a team in real time. This information is critical in dictating the cadence and strategy of the game from minute to minute. A football team that's down 28–3 early in the third quarter takes a very different approach to the game than one that's up 41–9 in the middle of the fourth quarter. The score and the game clock tell every player and coach how they should be playing the game every minute.

It would be absurd to think of trying to win a Super Bowl or World Series without the benefit of a scoreboard, and yet that is what many leaders attempt to do in business. They claim they want to win, but they fail to translate their business goals into specific, actionable numbers that everyone can observe and strive for. And they withhold vital information about the way the team is performing from the very "players" responsible for achieving victory. They think it's enough to just give their people a set of instructions and then pop their head in the door every third Tuesday of the month with a few words of criticism or encouragement.

That's not how you *make it happen* in business.

Employees are much better players when they always know the "score" in real time. What "inning" is it? What's my batting average or completion percentage? How many points do we need to score? Are we winning or losing? If we're losing, *why* are we losing? If we're winning, what are we doing right? How is our team doing compared to other teams? How am I doing as an individual player?

When people can see the scoreboard, they know well in advance of deadlines whether they are on track for a win or not; if not, they can start making adjustments to their performance sooner rather than later. The more information and feedback you can to give people minute by minute, the better they can tailor their energies in productive and efficient ways. On the other hand, when people are kept in the dark, they live in blissful ignorance—and that's hardly the ticket to a winning cadence.

In our company, as I've mentioned, we use an almost *literal* scoreboard. We hang a huge TV screen in a prominent location in the plant. On it we list our various departments—sales, manufacturing, mold tooling, corporate (finance), HR. We display our goals for each department by year and by month. We also list key measurables for each department. For example, for sales, we show things like percentage of on-time quotes, number of quotes per month, total new business booked for the month, and more. Next to the goal is either a green box or a red box. Green means you're meeting your goal; red means you're not.

		12/1/18	Q4 2018	JAN	FEB	MAR	Q1	GOAL
SALES	Quoted $$/Month	$15,057,014	$13,565,566	$1,215,065	$13,810,939	$11,331,270	$8,785,758	$3.5M
	Material Handling Quoted $$/month	$724,991	$914,327	$531,724	$2,411,810	$427,010	$1,123,515	$2.1M/M
	Lt. Weighting Quoted $$/month	$14,332,023	$12,651,239	$683,341	$11,309,129	$10,904,260	$7,632,243	$1.4M/M
	New Business Booked/Month	$466,379	$827,197	$856,701	$455,577	$5,555,398	$2,289,225	$1,500,000
	% On-Time Quotes	100%	96%	100%	100%	85%	95%	90%
	# Quotes/Month	25	27	32	32	24	28	30
	# Projects in the Building	68	65	68	72	70	70	≥40
MANUFACTURING	Top 5 Customer 1:PPM's	100	75	96	90	50	79	≤75
	Top 5 Customer 1: QPM Score	40	40	45	35	40	40	≤40
	Top 5 Customer 1: Delivery Ratings	95	96	92%	93%	95%	97%	≥98%
	Top 5 Customer 2 Delivery Ratings	25	25	24	24	25	24	25
	Top 5 Customer 2 Commercial Ratings	25	25	25	25	25	25	25
	Top 5 Customer 2 Quality Ratings	20	21	20	20	22	19	25
	Top 5 Customer Service Ratings	25	25	22	22	24	23	25
	Top 5 Customer 3 Delivery	99.4	99	96.5	94.2	91.4	94.0	98%
	Other Top 5 Customer delivery ratings	Customer A: 90% Customer B: 89% Customer C: 85% Customer D: 91% Customer F: 93%	Customer A: 90% Customer B: 89% Customer C: 85% Customer D: 91% Customer F: 93%	Customer A: 93% Customer B: 90% Customer C: 89% Customer D: 91% Customer F: 95%	Customer A: 91% Customer B: 88% Customer C: 92% Customer D: 95% Customer F: 96%	Customer A: 96% Customer B: 99% Customer C: 94% Customer D: 98% Customer F: 97%	Customer A: 96% Customer B: 99% Customer C: 94% Customer D: 98% Customer F: 97%	≥90%
	Total Waste cost %	2.96%	2.82%	3.15%	3.20%	2.61%	2.99%	<3%
	Component Labor OT%	9.0%	9%	11.0%	12.7%	12.2%	11.97%	7%
	Layered Process Audits:	Participation: 90% Compliance: 98%	Participation: 92% Compliance: 98%	Participation: 95% Compliance: 98%	Participation: 90% Compliance: 97%	Participation: 90% Compliance: 98%	Participation: 92% Compliance: 98%	100% 100%
CORPORATE	Sales	$2,858,700	$3,241,254	$3,369,000	$3,454,100	$4,087,000	$ 3,636,700.00	$2,503,000
	Site Gross Margin	37.1%	38%	38.9%	38.4%	39.5%	39%	30.0%
	Gross Margin Site	36.9%	36%	31.3%	32.1%	31.0%	31%	30.0%
	Days Inventory On Hand (DIOH)	39	38	38	39	40	39.0	~30
HR	Safety Incidents (Recordables)	0	0	0	0	0	$ -	0
	Lost Hours (Unplanned Time Off)	302	275	300	275	350	$ 308.67	<250 hours
	Total Direct Head Count	95	97	101.8	99.22	109.58	$ 103.53	Per schedule
	YTD Turn-Over (Salaried)	4%	3	0%	0%	0%	$ -	<12%
	YTD Turn-Over (Hourly)	4%	3	2%	4%	2%	3%	<29.1%

Just as in sports, the scoreboard tells us a lot, but it doesn't tell us everything. There are many intangibles as well. That's why every month we meet with the whole cross-functional team. In that meeting, everyone in charge of each metric has to explain *why* their metric is red or green and whether their green is sustainable or not. A red box, by the way, isn't necessarily a bad thing, and a green box isn't necessarily good. Sometimes it's okay to be red. Perhaps, for example, the manager of that metric had safety concerns and tells me, "I could have met my goal, but that would have compromised safety, and I wasn't going to do that." In that case, I'm glad to see a red. That manager is thinking about the long-term health of the company and his people—and I know that kind of thinking will eventually translate into winning numbers.

Your company might decide to use a different type of scoreboard from the one we use at MMI. That's fine; just make sure you use *some* kind of system that provides real-time feedback to everyone in the company. Plans and goals are only half the picture; the scoreboard is the other half. At MMI, for example, we take our annual plan and our SMART goals very seriously. But we know they only represent our game plan. The *scoreboard* is what tells us whether our game plan is working or whether we need to make some "halftime adjustments." A good game plan and a good scoreboard are both essential.

The scoreboard concept colors every interaction we have in our plant. I conduct at least weekly interfaces with all of my direct reports (who then have daily interfaces with all of their people). These meetings always focus on the scoreboard—our goals, our deadlines, our performance numbers. I carry a list of company goals around with me all the time, so I always know the score of the game every day. As we get closer to the end of the year, I can tell you whether we're on track to win or lose the game—and if it's the latter, I can start making adjustments to put us on track for a win. So there's never a surprise at the end of the year.

Here is a specific example of how the scoreboard helps us *make* it happen rather than *hope* for it to happen. One of our measurables is something called purchase price variance (PPV). Here's what it means: We buy a lot of parts and materials from outside suppliers, and we have a standard set up in our ERP system that tells us what each part is supposed to cost in order for us to stay within our target profit margin. If one of our suppliers starts raising their prices, we may find ourselves with a significant PPV, which means our cost to produce the associated product(s) will go up. And when that happens, our profitability will go down.

Because we're all able to clearly see our PPV in real time, we can start taking action if the number goes negative. That might mean a change in the way we hire, set our standards, or establish SMART goals for some of our key people. The mere practice of observing PPV as a key metric also affects the way we manage our supply base. For example, we often tell suppliers, "Once you've quoted us a price, you need to hold that price for the life of the program." We've also begun developing multiple sources for many of the products we buy, so that if the current supplier isn't meeting quality or price requirements, we can shift to another supplier. We've created supplier report cards for our supply base, too, so we can tell them, "Here's how we think you're doing. Your PPVs are in line. You're hitting our quality expectations." Or not.

The point is that we developed all these proactive interventions as a result of putting this particular measurable (PPV) on the scoreboard and keeping our eye on it, something we didn't do before we adopted our scoreboard system.

Your people are the beating heart of your company, but your scoreboard is your heart monitor. If you choose not to use one, your company might be flatlining, and you might not know it.

LEARN TO SAY NO

If I had to boil all of the leadership lessons I've learned over my entire career down to four simple words, they would be these: learn to say no. Learning to say no is the most difficult thing to do in a growing business, and yet it is a vital skill.

Everyone loves to say yes, me included. Why? Because it's fun to say yes. And when your company is starting to make money, it's tempting to say yes to a whole slew of new things. "Hey, let's buy that hot new piece of equipment!" "Hey, let's go call on that new customer because the product they make is so exciting!" "Hey, let's buy a new plant!" "Hey, let's hire some great new people!" "Hey, let's start a new product line!"

The more successful you are, the more opportunities come your way. You start to say to yourself, "I'm getting good at this. Now I can really grow my business." Pretty soon, you're growing in a dozen new directions, convinced that diversification is the path to even greater success. That's a huge fallacy. The truth is that if you don't stay focused on what you're good at, and on the customers you do your best work with, you will fail. You'll find yourself trying to be everything to everybody—and you'll end up being nothing to anyone.

When you take on too many new processes, new products, new customers, new industries, you're no longer focused in your approach. And staying focused is crucial. My advice is: do what you're good at, and do *only* what you're good at. Don't take on new customers and products just because you *can*.

Earlier in the book, I told you that one of the keys to my turning MMI around was learning to say no. When I came aboard at MMI, we were going after business in medical products, toys, packaging, automotive, heavy trucks, military, you name it. I was trying to be everything to everybody, and I was failing miserably. Every one of these customers, you see, had a different set of parameters, expectations, codes, and systems they wanted us to interface with. We could barely keep up, never mind gain expertise in all these areas.

A smarter approach is to choose customers who all have the same basic requirements so you can use the same systems over and over, duplicating your process for all your new customers.

Duplication is gold.

If you want to grow, it's more productive to do so with existing customers (if possible) than to keep adding new ones. If you *are* going to add new customers, you need to be sure they're a fit for your technologies, your know-how, your processes, your culture, your products, and your way of doing business. A lot of new customers will say, "Hey, we'll do business with you, but we need you to do much better on your pricing." And pretty soon, because you covet that particular customer, you find yourself working harder for less money—which is my definition of insanity.

Your regular, steady customers are the ones who have proven they recognize the value you provide and are willing to pay you fairly for that value. The secret to growth is not necessarily more products and more customers. Quite often, the secret is fewer products and fewer customers, but in greater quantities. Concentrate. Focus. Acquire mastery.

FOCUS ON YOUR HIGH-RETURN JOBS

The next management technique I'm going to share with you is closely related to the above one, but it gives you a specific tool to employ. The chart below, along with the corporate measurables chart (above), is one of the most powerful pieces of paper I use in running my business. I swear, this one chart gives me more valuable information than twelve Harvard MBA programs.

At the beginning of every month I do a "margin review" of all the products the company is currently working on. One purpose of this review is to continually identify where there is growth with each of our priority customers. The other purpose is to determine how best to allocate our attention and resources each month. The latter part is critical. Let me explain.

[Perhaps insert a graphic of the Margin Review chart here.]

At the top of this chart you will see a list of twenty jobs called "Largest Revenue Items." At any given time, we're probably working on four to five hundred different products at MMI. This list shows the top twenty of them in terms of revenue generation. These are the products and projects that are currently bringing the most money in the door.

In the bottom-right corner of the top-twenty list, you'll see a percentage number. This number shows the percentage of our *total revenue* that these twenty jobs represent. Typically, this number is around two-thirds. That's hugely significant—it means that, as a general rule, the bulk of our revenue is coming from only the top twenty jobs out of four or five hundred. So what I tell my operators is, "If you do those top twenty jobs well, the numbers for the month will take care of themselves." To put it more crudely, "You can screw up the other four hundred jobs, and we'll still come out on top." Not that we would ever do that, but you get the point.

It's sort of a corollary to the 80–20 rule—you need to spend 80 percent of your time focusing on your top-producing jobs, rather than spreading your attention across hundreds of tasks that amount to minutiae. Focus on the key jobs. That's how you leverage your people and processes.

Below the top list on the chart are two more lists that are extremely critical. The middle list shows our ten *most profitable* jobs, in terms of gross margin (GM). Finally, the bottom list shows our ten worst-performing jobs in terms of margin.

When I look at the highest-margin (most profitable) jobs, I immediately check to see if some of these jobs are also appearing on my top list, the revenue producers. Ideally, what I want to see is a lot of our highest-margin jobs appearing on the top-twenty list for revenue as well. What that indicates is that our biggest revenue producers are also the ones giving us the highest profits. That's when your business is in the sweet spot.

Conversely, what you *don't* want to see is jobs from your *lowest*-margin list appearing in the top-twenty revenue-producers list. Because that indicates that a big chunk of your revenue is failing to turn a decent profit. Or in other words, you're increasing your top line without increasing your bottom line. Not good.

But either way, the great news is that this chart gives you the information you need to act. It tells you, "Here are some jobs we need to fix, or we're going to see poor results for the month"—or, as I like to put it, "We can see the train coming now, and we know when it's going to hit us." Which means we can start taking action to reroute the train.

So this one piece of paper tells my team exactly which jobs to focus on and where to make improvements. It's like getting a peek at the score of the game before the game has been played. This piece of paper also tells us which customers—and which jobs associated with those customers—are the best ones for our company. So we know what kinds of jobs to go after when we're seeking new business in the future.

This powerful sheet of paper is a vital component of our scoreboard system. And do you know how many man-hours it takes me to produce this chart every month? Zero. The system spits it out automatically. The power of metrics.

KEEP YOUR INTERNAL FOCUS TIGHT

As important as it is to say no to new customers, new product lines, new industries, and new facilities, it is equally important to say no to too many internal initiatives. It's crucial, especially in a growing company, not to try to take on too many goals and foci at once. Organizational focus has its limits. People can only juggle so many goals at a time. If you throw too many objectives at people at once, none of them will take root.

That's why every year I focus on no more than ten goals for the company. As I'm preparing my operating plan every year, I think of dozens of goals I *want* to achieve, and all of them seem important and worthy. But I know I can't tackle them all at once. Some goals will have to wait. I know if we try to do more than ten things—and even ten is a lot—we'll lose sight of several of our goals, and we'll fail at others. I want a record of success, not failure.

Change needs to come at a pace at which it can be absorbed. Otherwise, you will overwhelm people. That's why, for example, when we first started doing performance reviews at MMI, we decided to take it in stages. No one at the company had had a performance review in years, and people's attitudes were very negative about the idea. We knew this was going to be a major change for the organization, so I told the director of HR to go gentle the first year and to keep the reviews simple and positive the first time around.

You need to get to know your team before you can know how many changes it will be able to absorb and at what speed. And change always needs to be measured, manageable, and digestible.

BE SCALABLE, BE SUSTAINABLE

One of the things I tell my management team all the time is, "I don't want to be lucky; I want to be good." In other words, I'm not interested in getting great results that are a fluke; I'm interested in getting great results that are repeatable and sustainable.

One of the surest ways to get sustainable results is to create standardized processes you can duplicate to produce the same results over and over. When I was trying to find ways to improve standardization at MMI, I looked to the king of standardization: McDonald's. (A wise manager doesn't just look within his/her own industry for ideas, but also looks at completely unrelated businesses.)

McDonald's became the exemplar for scalability by creating a process and a workflow design that could be replicated thousands of times over for the exact same results. The appeal of McDonald's is that customers always know exactly what to expect whenever they see the Golden Arches anywhere in the world. They know they're always going to get the same "two all-beef patties, special sauce, lettuce, cheese, pickles, onions on a sesame seed bun." Right?

McDonald's achieved scalability by finding the best efficiencies for building a hamburger and then standardizing that process. Each shop uses the same equipment, set up in the same way, and the same ingredients and steps. The cheeseburger slides down the same little chute in Des Moines, Iowa, as it does in Saint Petersburg, Russia. Every McDonald's restaurant buys the same supplies from the same set of suppliers. Anyone who's worked in one McDonald's is automatically trained to work in all of them.

All of this allows McDonald's franchisers to control and predict their costs, their employee training, and their product output, whether they own one McDonald's or fifty of them.

I want to achieve some of the same sustainability and scalability in my business, so I borrow many of the same ideas. I spend a lot of time on my work floor, trying to create the most efficient workflow with each type of work cell. And then I standardize it. Every work cell uses the same type of equipment and has the same work table with the same tools and the same signage, all set up the same way. I even standardize from plant to plant. If you walk into any of my facilities, you'll see the exact same equipment, set up the same way. Workers have the same computer read-out screens, programmed the same way.

As a result, when I go to quote any new product, I know exactly what the process will be and how that product will flow through the plant. I know my documented costs, and I have a very good idea of how much time the job's going to take, which operators I'll need to put on which cells, and what my profitability is going to be. Hope is not my plan.

REINVEST, DON'T CASH OUT

When it comes to building a sustainable business, there's another important principle to keep in mind. You must resist the temptation to "cash out" on your business. What do I mean by that?

Wherever you're at, you're not good enough. There's always opportunity to improve.

Well, a lot of owners and leaders in business become seduced by the lure of immediate profits. They want to show the biggest numbers they can, *right now*. Instead of focusing on building a profitable, sustainable business for the long term, they look for the quick payout, which they try to achieve by tapping out their resources.

I've seen business owners who work their people twelve or fifteen hours a day, without investing in them, paying them appropriately, or doing things like having luncheons with them or giving them bonuses and awards. They just want to put all the money back into their own pocket and say, "Look how great I'm doing." In the long run, this approach always fails. If you take too much without giving in return, you burn your people out, and you lose them.

There have been times I've been tempted to say, "We don't have enough money this year to hand out bonuses—that will hamper our ability to buy capital equipment." But then I've thought long and hard about it and realized, "That's not right. I don't want to grow my business at the expense of my people. Because if my people aren't here, it doesn't matter how much equipment I have. I need to invest in my people."

Owners often try to cash out on the capital end too. They'll say, "Hey, I took a loan out to buy that machine. I had a five-year term note on it, and I just finished paying it off. And you know what? That machine is still running fine. It'll probably run for a long time. I'll just pocket that money for a few years, instead of investing it back into new equipment."

In my case, I spend millions of dollars a year investing in capital equipment. For example, I buy these huge injection-molding machines. They might cost a million dollars or more apiece, and I'll use them for many years, so I amortize them over many years.

Let's say a given molding machine has a useful life of fifteen years. At fifteen years, I will replace it. Period. I don't care if it's my best-running machine on the floor. I will replace it because I know that if I keep running it, at some point it's going to cause me a *big* problem. There's always a temptation to say, "I could show a million dollars more in profitability this year if I *don't* buy that piece of equipment." As the owner of the company, I know I could put a million bucks in my pocket and go buy a boat or a new house. But that kind of thinking doesn't align with long-term profitability and sustainability.

Never cash out on the business. Always look to invest into your equipment and your people.

NEVER BECOME SUPERIOR

It's essential to celebrate your company's achievements, but it's also essential never to adopt a feeling of superiority, or to buy into the belief that you've "made it."

Wherever you're at, you're not good enough. There's always opportunity to improve.

The day before I wrote these words, for example, I looked at my company's total performance for the first quarter of this year as compared to the first quarter of last year. We grew an astonishing 53 percent, year over year, and our profitability was double what we'd forecasted it to be. Those are great numbers—fantastic, really—but they are also dangerous ones. The temptation is to pat myself on the back and put the business on cruise control. Instead, I had one of the most difficult conversations I've ever had with my team and my CFO. I told them, "No matter how good you think we are, we have many areas we need to improve on."

I showed the team several places where we were throwing money away. "As well as we did," I pointed out, "we had one of the worst performances operationally that we've ever had." That may sound strange, given our overall performance numbers, but if you looked at metrics such as the number of days we had inventory on hand or our cash-conversion cycles, you would see that we hadn't really been hitting our benchmarks. And if you analyzed what we spent on raw materials versus where the market was, you'd see we'd missed out on opportunities to buy materials at a much lower price. Had we done those things right, our performance could have been even better.

If you ever watch Bill Belichick after a Patriots win, you'll notice that he congratulates the team and lets them savor their victory for a few minutes, and then he starts focusing on the things the team could have done better, the points they left on the field, and starts looking ahead to the next game. He never allows the team to feel complacent or superior, despite its historically high win rate. That's how he has been able to create a winning culture for two decades. As a leader, you need to do the same thing. You tell everybody they did a good job, and you buy them dinner, but you also say, "Here are the areas we need to focus on going forward, because we can do a lot better." When you communicate that way, you create a culture of continuous improvement.

When people think they're at the top of the mountain, they get lax. They become a bit arrogant. That's why I cringe when I see or hear companies—in their marketing materials and internal communications—use phrases like "We have superior technology," or "We offer superior quality," or just plain old "We're superior." I hate the word *superior*, and I'll never use it in my business. When you think you're superior, you lose the ability to grow. You feel no need to work harder, work smarter, or improve. That's detrimental to a business, and frankly, it's boring too. The idea that there is always room for growth gives me energy. It gives me passion. It gives me excitement. I never get bored, nor does anybody around me. Why? Because the relentless pursuit of excellence is fun!

CHAPTER 8

COACHING, MENTORING, LEADING

We talked in chapter 7 about the importance of scalability. If you want to grow your business, you must find ways to create efficiencies and standardize your processes so that these processes can be duplicated over and over, with relatively little specialized management. McDonald's became McDonald's because its processes were duplicable.

But there is one element in your business that is extremely challenging to duplicate: you.

At some point, you are going to need to find ways to replicate the leadership, knowledge, and management skills you bring to the table so that everything in the company isn't running through you personally. You will need to develop other leaders, trained in your mold, who can take over departments, plants, and even whole divisions of companies. You will need to multiply yourself by three times, five times, ten times, or even more. And the leaders you develop will also need to be capable of duplicating *themselves*.

When everything is running through you, the growth of the company remains stunted. Only when you actively work toward replicating yourself can the company begin to multiply in exponential ways.

I have seen leaders who have failed to do this. I knew one individual, for example, who was very good at his job. He had the *skills* to coach and mentor others, but he couldn't get out of his own way. He wanted to control everything, and so he "built a moat" around himself. He made sure not to tell anyone too much. That way, everyone had to go to him to get answers. He thought this would ensure his continued importance and value to the company. But, in fact, his worth eventually went down because he refused to develop other leaders.

In a growing company, the true value of leaders lies in their willingness and ability to duplicate themselves—because that is what a growing company needs: a steady stream of new leaders and managers. And the only way that result can be achieved is through consistent and repeated coaching and mentoring. Coaching and mentoring must be an integral part of the culture you create as a leader.

> *Coaching, mentoring, and leading are not occasional remedial activities. Rather, they are an integral part of the daily pulsebeat of the company.*

Even if you're not interested in growing your company (at least for the moment), coaching and mentoring are essential for the health of the business. Why? Two good reasons. First of all, you need to develop people who can step up in your absence in the event you are run over by a bus. Second, you need to continually educate, refine, and develop your managers and front-line staff so that you can hold on to them. People get restless when they stand still for too long. Unless employees are given opportunities to grow, attrition will be the eventual result.

So whether you want to grow your company or not, a constant investment in your people through coaching, mentoring, and leadership is crucial.

INDEPENDENCE IS OVERRATED

We live in a nation and a culture that has always cherished independence. The models we're told to emulate are rugged individualists like frontiersmen (and women), explorers, rebels, underdogs, and self-made millionaires. And that's great, of course. The spirit of independence is a beautiful thing. But there's a danger in taking it too far, in believing that we alone possess all the answers and all the skills. In fact, no man is an island, and we are all better human beings and better leaders when we learn from others and pass our knowledge along to those who are following behind us. The collective mind is smarter and wiser than the individual mind.

This has been a hard lesson for me to learn. Watching my mother go out and work hard to earn the things she wanted for her family gave me a tremendous sense of self-motivation and self-discipline, as I've mentioned. By the time I was eighteen, I was running my own landscaping business, going to school full time, and working full time. And I thought the way I had to do all that was to be tough-minded and independent.

College taught me an important lesson in that regard. My over-stuffed schedule kept me extremely busy, so I didn't have time to mess around and wait on others to do things. For the first two years of college, I did all my homework alone at home. To my surprise, however, I found myself struggling to get decent grades. I couldn't figure out why I was unable to grasp the material better and perform better on tests.

It wasn't until my third year that I developed some on-campus friends and classmates I could study with. Suddenly I was able to gather inputs from others whenever I was struggling to understand something. I developed a help network to support me in better understanding my schoolwork and knowing what to expect from my professors. My performance in school dramatically improved, and I rose to the top of my classes.

In short, I learned the value of teamwork and getting coaching/mentoring from others. My own throughput and the quality of my work went up exponentially. Most of all, I discovered that I enjoyed the teamwork and camaraderie.

Early in my professional career, I also had to learn to share decision-making. When I entered the workforce, I was determined to get results. I didn't care who was in my way. I wanted to get where I wanted to go, and I would steamroll over anyone who wasn't fully on board with me.

I learned the hard way that when people are run over, they feel undervalued and unimportant—and, oh by the way, they don't feel much affection for the person who's running them over. Not only did I need to learn to *take input* from others, but I also needed to learn to *give output* to others, so that they could be informed and empowered enough to participate in the decision-making process.

Bottom line: a company is an infinitely stronger organization when there is a constant and dynamic exchange of knowledge through coaching, mentoring, and leading.

COACHING, MENTORING, AND LEADING— WHAT'S THE DIFFERENCE?

Coaching, mentoring, and leading are not occasional remedial activities. Rather, they are an integral part of the daily pulsebeat of the company. As a leader, you need to constantly coach, mentor, and lead those directly under you, and also make sure the company employs a robust system of coaches, mentors, teachers, and trainers, so that everyone, at every level of the company, is benefiting from being coached and taught.

You may find yourself doing all three of these activities— coaching, mentoring, and leading—on a daily basis, and sometimes they overlap one another in such a way that they are virtually indistinguishable. But they are three distinct activities.

COACHING

A coach, essentially, is someone who has the playbook and teaches it regularly and continuously. A coach knows the goals of the company and how the company operates. A coach also knows the players— their strengths, their weaknesses, their challenges. A coach helps each individual player make his or her most valuable contribution to the team.

People look to coaches for direction, for know-how, for the pathway to get to where they need to go. Coaches help set the cadence for the company.

A coach may point out specific things an employee needs to work on and plot a path to getting there. For example, if an individual is rubbing coworkers the wrong way, the coach might try to help this employee gain insight into his/her social skills and might give him or her some communication exercises to work on. A coach does a lot of direct teaching.

A mix of both internal and external coaching is ideal. Inside coaches—coaches who work within the company—are valuable because they have a personal investment in winning and because they know the ins and outs of the company culture better than outsiders. Outside coaches are equally critical because they can see situations objectively, and because they bring in new skills and knowledge. For example, I've been using a third-party sales coach for many years because of the value he brings. Employees often feel better about getting advice from someone who will not judge them and has no skin in the game. They can use an outside coach to rehearse how they will approach a challenging customer scenario or management encounter. My sales team has their coach's cell number and can call him anytime for quick advice.

Sometimes I'll bring in outside coaches/trainers if I need expertise in a certain area. For example, I was recently having some issues with quality and throughput in a particular part of the manufacturing floor. I brought in an outside consultant/trainer to train my staff on how to improve their processes. Via the training, I was also able to identify an issue I hadn't been aware of before. The trainer reported to me that everyone who took the training had been engaged and energetic, except for one person who seemed to feel the training was beneath him. The trainer tested everyone before and after the training on the skills being taught and, tellingly enough, the one person whose skills did not improve was the person who had the superior attitude. This individual tested lowest before the training and lowest afterward. Bringing in an outside eye was what allowed me to uncover this employee problem and address it.

What makes a good coach? Good coaches are always positive in their approach. They coach people up, never put them down. They clearly communicate what a "win" is for the team and what each individual needs to accomplish in order to score that win.

CRITIQUING THE COACH

Coaches should *never* feel they are above being coached themselves or evaluating their processes to ensure those processes are producing the best results. Recently, I have been reviewing one department in my business that has had significant performance issues and personnel turnover. Knowing that unemployment rates are at a fifty-year low and that it is extremely difficult to find good people, I heard myself saying, "We just can't find good people to do the job we need in this tight labor market." I decided it was time for a process check!

I went to our human resources department and requested copies of the job descriptions and training plans for the problematic positions. I also took the opportunity to sit down with a few of our struggling employees to ask them some questions about specific job tasks they face on a daily basis. Many of our newer employees gave me a blank stare in response and could not really articulate what the correct process was. I was able to confirm that these struggling employees had not had several of our core processes addressed in their training plan. Meanwhile, we were spending hours writing coaching letters and employee write-ups while enduring poor performance, turnover, recruiting fees, and damage to our customer rapport.

I was reminded of the old phrase "garbage in, garbage out." How could we expect to see top performances, great results, and highly motivated, long-term employees when we were not coaching/training people properly? You can't yell at the receiver for not running the right pass route when you never gave him the playbook!

Human resources *are* hard to come by these days, so make sure you invest in them properly. I can't emphasize enough: only when you train your people in what they need to know can you expect results. We have greatly improved employee morale and retention by continuing to check our processes to ensure our most important resources are being coached properly.

MENTORING

A mentor's role can overlap a bit with a coach's but is different. Mentors are seasoned individuals whom people trust and go to when they need confidential guidance. Mentors offer advice and present possible solutions with an attitude of, "Here's what I did when I was in a similar position." Mentors are fully on the side of their mentees and may offer advice on how to deal with management as well as how to work *with* management. They offer a sounding board. Their posture is not so much, "Here's what you need to do and how to do it," but rather, "Here's another way of looking at things."

Sometimes mentors are *not* in leadership positions—at least within the mentee's company. They may be outsiders too. People can confide in mentors because they don't feel as if they're putting their own professional well-being at risk by admitting, for example, that they don't know how to do an assigned task or that maybe they screwed something up.

Often a mentor is a slightly older, wiser, more experienced person, someone who's "been there, done that." People often find their own mentors. They may gravitate toward someone inside or outside the company whom they particularly like, admire, and/or trust. These natural mentorships are terrific, but they don't always occur. So the leadership team should make sure there are mentorship opportunities available to all employees.

Good mentors possess certain key qualities. First and foremost, they care about the individuals they are mentoring and have a keen interest in getting to know them. They always have their mentees' long-term success in mind. Mentors possess emotional intelligence, which allows them to help their mentees navigate difficult interpersonal situations. Mentors listen first and give advice later. And mentors are vulnerable and human—they open up about their own past mistakes and allow their mentees to learn from them.

LEADERS

If a coach is the person who teaches to the playbook, then a leader is the person who writes the playbook. A good leader holds the vision for the company. He or she has a well-thought-out plan and is able to articulate every phase of it. A good leader sticks to the plan and doesn't change course continually. The role of a leader is to inspire people to believe in the plan, to encourage them to stick to it, and to provide rewards and recognition when the team employs the plan successfully.

I can't say I had a lot of exposure to great leadership when I was coming up. My models were mostly negative. I developed my own leadership style in reaction to their leadership failures, which I was determined not to duplicate. I did have one positive leader/mentor, however. He was the founder of the first company I worked for after college. He started his business in his proverbial garage and built it on a foundation of treating people the way you want to be treated. If you're loyal to people, they will be loyal to you in return. This leader built a substantial company full of people who had endless loyalty to him and to the business. I then watched his successor come in and take the exact opposite approach. And I saw the company fall apart as a result. That was an extremely powerful lesson for me.

We've been talking throughout this book about characteristics I believe are required of good leaders—qualities such as passion, accountability, self-knowledge, good communications, and a willingness to walk the talk and set the cadence. In addition to these qualities, great leaders also need to understand that their role is to serve the business, not to serve themselves or abuse their power. *Service* is the key word here. True leaders know that their own goals will be met only after the business has been served. A selfish leader may do well in the short term but will fail in the long run.

Great leaders don't try to do everything themselves; they give people the space to make mistakes and to learn from them. This is a very difficult skill for many leaders to learn. After all, they often *became* leaders because they have an alpha personality, a hunger to get ahead, and an ability to get things done. It is in their very nature to want to be holding the steering wheel. But good leaders know they must let others take the wheel sometimes. Because if a team sees that its leader is always going to step in, they'll take the approach of, "Why should I do it myself? He's just going to jump in and do it for me. I'll just let him take the risk."

The ideal leadership scenario is a little bit like a drivers' ed car with two sets of driver controls. As the leader, you let the other person drive the car as much as possible, but if you see them heading for a crash, you seize the wheel. You later explain to them why you did it, and you give them another chance down the road to get it right.

A great leader is humble enough to learn from his/her team and from others outside the company. If someone else comes up with a way of doing things that is superior to the leader's, the leader is able to put his or her ego on hold and do what is best for the company.

Ultimately that might even include stepping aside as the leader if a more capable person comes along. A true leader, when confronted with his or her own limitations, ought to be able to say, "I've grown the company as large and strong as I can with my particular talents. Maybe it's time to bring in some fresh blood or promote X to CEO. Or maybe it's time to merge with a company that has much more experience in this market." Some leaders, such as Jeff Bezos, have been able to continue to lead their company, no matter how large it gets. And that's great. But it's also fairly rare. There is great virtue in caring enough about a company to step aside if you no longer believe you are the best person in the world to run it.

GUIDELINES FOR ALL COACHES, MENTORS, AND LEADERS

Though coaching, mentoring, and leading are distinct skills and activities, there are certain practices and principles that all good coaches, mentors, and leaders should keep in mind.

COACHING AND TEACHING SHOULDN'T BE AN OCCASIONAL THING

Many leaders bring in coaches and mentors only as special interventions, when something needs fixing. But this approach is wildly inadequate, in my opinion. Can you imagine if the coach of a sports team took that attitude? Imagine if they sent their team off to play a series in some faraway city and said, "Here's my number; call me if you need me"? That would be absurd. A sports team needs coaching every day, both in practices and in real games.

Business teams are no different. People require ongoing guidance and support to bring out their A game every day. They need to know how they are doing, how the company is doing, and how they fit into the picture. A coach's job is to show everyone the scoreboard and translate it into motivated action on a daily basis.

That is why coaching and mentoring, like good communication, must be regular and continuous. And everyone in the company must take part. That means the leadership team and the HR office must look at every single employee in the company and ask, "Where, when, and how is this individual receiving regular coaching and mentoring?" And they must provide good answers.

CONSTRUCTIVE CONFLICT

Whether you're a leader, a mentor, or a coach—or a combination of all three—sooner or later (usually sooner) you will find yourself in conflict with an employee or group whose performance is not in line with where the company needs to be going. Conflict is fine; it can be a springboard for growth. But conflict must be handled constructively. *Constructive* conflict means sitting down with a person or a group and talking in positive terms about what needs to change in order for the company to reach its goals. Constructive conflict is always goal oriented.

You don't call someone out in front of others and say, "You're doing a lousy job, idiot." That (in case you didn't notice) is an example of negative and nonconstructive conflict. Rather, you focus on what the business needs. And then, based on the needs of the business, you ask, "What does this individual or department need to do in order to serve the business?"

The rule we try to follow at my company is: If the issue at hand is something that involves multiple people, we address it with the group. We'll tell them, for example, "Here's what the business needs. Here's where we currently are with our results. We're not achieving what we need to. So we need to change what we're doing. Let's figure it out." That's constructive.

If it's a single individual who's having an issue, we will take that person aside and speak to them in private. Again, the focus is on goals, not on personal attacks. As an example, let's look at that employee I mentioned above who had the negative attitude toward training. We spoke to him in private and presented the facts to him without accusation or anger. "So here were your scores before the training, and here are your scores after. They're the lowest in the group. We offered a training for the group, and the trainer tells us you felt the training was beneath you. Something doesn't jibe here. You believe you're the most skilled person on the team, but the data shows us you're the least. We want to invest in you and train you, but we need to get to reality in a hurry. Are you willing to do that with us?"

GETTING TO "I DON'T KNOW" IS A VICTORY

Whatever form of teaching or leading you are doing, the most productive place you can arrive at is when someone admits they don't know how to do something and needs help. When that occurs, the individual becomes open and receptive to teaching, training, and leading. You can now work with this person.

As we've discussed before, most workers are reluctant to admit they don't know something. They think this makes them look bad, and they worry it might put their job security at risk. So they hide their lack of knowledge and try to *look* good rather than *be* good.

It's essential that all leaders, mentors, and coaches at a company work together to create a culture in which admitting you need help is celebrated, not condemned. This takes time, because people's natural inclination is to be self-protective. But if you consistently reward and acknowledge people who have the courage to ask for help, you will change your culture over time.

There are a couple of types of "I don't know" that don't fall into the above category. One is the "I don't know" of someone who *has* been fully trained but who has chosen to remain disengaged from their training. This person, by all rights, *should* know the skills or information by now but has shut their mind off to it. It's a very different conversation you need to have with this person.

The other "I don't know" you may encounter as a leader or coach is that of the person who doesn't know what they want to do career-wise. Often you get this response when you sit down to talk to people, especially millennials, about their future goals. You sense they're becoming restless career-wise, but when you ask them what they want to do, they say, "I don't know." The reason they give this answer may be that no one has ever asked them before or because the question is too open-ended for them. It's wise, therefore, as you enter a career discussion like this, to have some specific training and advancement suggestions in mind that you can offer. When people hear specifics, they are often able to engage in the discussion in a more meaningful way. You should also emphasize that in order for you to help them meet their career goals, you need to hear from them regularly about what they honestly want.

ADVANCEMENT ISN'T ALWAYS THE BEST THING

It's important to realize, as you're developing new leaders and trying to duplicate yourself by three times or five times, that advancement isn't always the right answer. Not everyone *wants* to be a leader or to take on new responsibilities. Sometimes you have good people who are doing a good job in their roles, and it's okay to leave them there.

There was one individual at my company, for example, who was a great employee, and I thought he had terrific leadership potential. So I approached him with what I thought was an impressive training package to help groom him as a future leader. His response was surprising to me: "I don't know why you're pushing that on me. That's not what I want." I think I eventually pushed this person out of the company because I tried to take him places he didn't want to go.

When you're offering people a path to leadership, you need to make sure it's a two-way street. The career move needs to be good for the company *and* for the individual. If it isn't right for both parties, it isn't going to work.

COACHING AND MENTORING ARE 24-7 JOBS

Finally, there is one essential truth to keep in mind about being a coach, mentor, and/or leader. That is, the job never stops. You may think your role ends when you finish a teaching or coaching session, but the fact is that people are watching you 24–7. They're picking up ideas, habits, and approaches by observing your "offstage" words and actions—the way you walk around the office, the way you behave at meetings, the way you interact with peers and underlings. You are *always* teaching—even when you're not teaching. As with being a parent, the behavior you *model* is far more important than the behavior you *teach*.

This even extends to how you act and present yourself outside of work—the way you treat waiters in restaurants, the way you dress when you go to the supermarket, and, nowadays, the way you behave on social media. The latter is especially important. You mustn't be involved in online activities or groups that reflect poorly on your character or show any kind of prejudices or questionable ethics. You can't expect people to take you seriously as a leader if you post pictures of yourself throwing up at keg parties or posing seminaked. You need to choose an exemplary set of values and live by them *all the time*. Being a leader and mentor is a 24–7 job.

YOU NEED COACHING AND MENTORING TOO

In the end, all the coaching and mentoring in the world won't get your company anywhere unless you, too, are receiving constant teaching and feedback. You need to be continually growing as a person and a leader and making sure your decision-making is grounded by a good set of checks and balances.

Personally, I surround myself with coaches and mentors. I regularly consult with a strong team of advisers, both inside and outside the company. For example, as I mentioned earlier, I have a sales coach I've worked with for over fifteen years. He doesn't just talk to my sales team—he talks to *me*—about approaching business development, winning new customers, handling difficult negotiations, and more. I bring in manufacturing experts who review my operations by walking my manufacturing floor on a regular basis. I employ industry consultants who look at everything we do at MMI, from financial tracking/performance to tax planning to corporate structure to human resource planning/training. I have strong legal counsel that helps me with business planning and business succession planning. I rely on Plante Moran to provide me with good industry benchmarks to shoot for.

I also make sure there is strong leadership *under* me who will call me out if I stray from the plan. These are my company "generals," and I rely on them for reality checks. I make it clear to everyone on my management team that I'm not looking for yes people. I want people who will step up and challenge me if my thinking is out of whack.

Right now MMI is doing a lot of forecasting for the next five years of our business, and I recently put together a comprehensive forecast model. I've been talking to my bank about it, and everybody seems happy with it, but I still made the decision to bring in an outside consulting team. I've tasked these consultants with building their own model, using similar inputs to what I've been using. I want to see how their model comes out, and I'm spending a substantial amount of money to get this done. Why? Because I want someone with no skin in the game to tell me whether or not they believe in the investments I'm making for the future. I trust myself, but I know I have blind spots and biases.

A culture of constant learning and improvement is what keeps a company vibrant and moving forward. It's your job as a leader to create this kind of culture, day in and day out.

SUCCESS TODAY AND TOMORROW

M y enthusiasm for the ideas I've been presenting in this book is off the charts. I have high confidence that if you take these ideas for a test drive, you will see your business gaining traction, speed, and direction like never before. And your potential will be unlimited.

But of course, my opinion is a tad biased. If the facts—as well as the opinions of people who work for MMI, do business with MMI, and analyze the company objectively—didn't back me up, you could toss this book in the reject pile along with *Lose Thirty Pounds in Four Hours* and *Make Your First Million without Getting Out of Bed*.

Fortunately, the validation for what we've been doing at MMI *has* been coming in—from all directions.

> *The opinions that mean the most to me, bar none, are those of our customers. Our entire reason for existing as a business is to please our customers and create a compelling value proposition for them.*

CUSTOMERS

The opinions that mean the most to me, bar none, are those of our customers. Our entire reason for existing as a business is to please our customers and create a compelling value proposition for them. As I've noted, when I first took the reins of MMI, we were not topping any customers' favorites lists. We had a reputation for being poor in communicating, late on delivering, and rather uninterested in our customers' thoughts.

This poor-to-lukewarm reputation was extremely distressing to me, and I immediately set out to change it. Of all the notable reversals we've made at MMI, the one of which I am proudest is the change in the way our customers think of us.

You may recall, early in the book, I shared with you the story of Jim, a particularly tough-minded customer who was thoroughly skeptical about my promises to do a better job for him and his company. I made a commitment to use Jim as my new benchmark—I knew that if I could turn Jim around, it would mean I'd made a quantum leap, not only in my customer relations, but in my company's progress as a whole.

My team and I went to work doing just that. We made sure we paid special attention to all the jobs we did for Jim's company and met all of our commitments to him as well as improved our communications. After a year had passed following our first in-person meeting, I called Jim and asked him if we could meet again. We sat down together, and I said, "A year ago you told me you were unhappy with our company's performance. I've been working diligently since then to make some changes, and I'm wondering if you have seen a difference."

Jim let out a grumble and finally acknowledged, "You guys *are* doing a lot better. I haven't had any complaints for a while, and frankly I'm surprised."

This was high praise coming from Jim. He is not a person prone to bubbly enthusiasm. In fact, you might say he hands out compliments like they're manhole covers. So for him to offer these comments was an amazing victory. I said, "On a scale of one to ten, where would you rate us now?"

Jim thought for a few moments and then said, "About a seven, I guess."

For Jim to offer a seven was like anyone else offering a 22.5. I thanked him for his candid comments and told him to stay tuned. There were more improvements, products, and services on the way, I assured him.

Another year passed, and we were hosting an open house at the plant to show off some of our new technologies. Jim showed up, along with about twenty-eight people who worked under him. I remember I was standing in a large gathering room when his group came in, and Jim spotted me from across the room. He approached me with his hand out, took me aside, and said, "Hey, I gotta talk to you." I was all ears. "You came to see me two years ago, and I was skeptical. I'd watched a lot of people before you making promises, and they didn't keep any of them. Well ... I don't know how you did it, but I have *never* seen a company turn around like yours has. In just two years, you've gone from being a supplier we were ready to fire to being the best-performing supplier we have. I wanted to shake your hand and say thank you for that."

His words literally brought tears to my eyes. Since then, we have heard the same kind of statement from many of our customers. I'll give you one more example.

A few years ago, I organized my team to go after Navistar as a customer. We spent a *lot* of time getting our foundation in place to qualify us to supply Navistar. When the time was right, we pursued an opportunity to develop business there. I personally spent almost two years working on this Navistar project, which we ultimately lost to a competitor. I felt terrible for my team for losing this business, which we had worked so hard to win, and which, frankly, we *deserved* to win. We had actually developed all the designs the company ended up using.

I flew to Navistar's headquarters to talk to the purchasing manager about this situation. Fortunately, she had done her research before I arrived. She knew I was upset and feeling slighted. Upon my arrival at the meeting, she took the proverbial knife out of my hand and said, "Before you get started, I want you to know I met with the engineering team, and they raved about your company's support and innovation." She went on to say, "We made a mistake in awarding that business to another company. The reason we did it was that the purchasing team didn't know your guys, but I promise you I will make this right."

She was as good as her word. Before leaving the meeting, I received an opportunity to quote a substantial package of new parts to Navistar. Within two weeks of my visit, the purchasing manager called me herself to award us the business. After eighteen months of work, we had not only launched all of the new products, but we had also become the go-to supplier for plastics products for Navistar. We had delivered on every promise!

At about the eighteen-month mark, I received a phone call from the director of purchasing, and he told me that the entire purchasing and engineering team had nominated MMI for their Diamond Supplier Award, which is given only to their top supplier. They explained that as a rule no company can even be *eligible* for the award until after three years of supplying parts, but when it had come time for nominations, MMI was the first name out of everyone's mouth.

A prestigious awards dinner came along with the Diamond Supplier designation. When I walked into the room, the original purchasing manager was awaiting my arrival. She greeted me and said, "Wow, only eighteen months in, and you receive our top supplier award. I knew I made a good choice when I met with you and gave you a second chance." Amazing and humbling.

Customer satisfaction means everything to me. The way we formerly measured it was by sending out annual surveys to hundreds of customers and awaiting their responses. When you do this, you get a handful of surveys returned if you're lucky, so you end up evaluating your customer satisfaction based on a 1 or 2 percent response rate. Perfectly useless.

Today we measure customer satisfaction by asking ourselves the following: Are we getting new quote opportunities? Are we winning new work? Do we have good quality and delivery ratings? If all of these things are happening, that means customers are satisfied. But most of all, we *talk to customers directly*. And we *listen* to them. We may not always like everything we hear, but it's only when we hear criticism that we gain opportunities to perform even better. Without asking the hard questions and listening to customers' answers, we might be delivering 80 percent satisfaction. We want to be as close to 100 percent as humanly possible.

OUR PEOPLE

The way our own people feel about the company is just as important as how our customers feel. I'll let them speak for themselves. Here is a small sampling of statements from a variety of people who have seen the company up close—as employees, suppliers, and colleagues.

> *What attracts me to MMI: the ever-changing and consistent growth ... forward-thinking ideas such as a wellness program and unique work processes. What inspires me about MMI: seeing the vast change over the last several years, and the accomplishments the organization has achieved since I started.*
>
> **Ernie**
> *(MMI employee)*

> *MMI's growth makes it feel like a start-up, with all the energy and activity of a start-up. This growth means I am always busy and continually looking at how to improve HR offerings as we grow. I enjoy the controlled autonomy you provide to me as a leader. While it's not "anything goes," you allow me to explore new options that will improve HR service delivery or improve the company culture.*
>
> **Ed**
> *(director of HR at MMI)*

Why MMI? I have been around MMI for the last four years. As an outside supplier, I have seen double-digit growth happen year after year. I have seen a company that invests in its people. A growing company that invests in its people—that's a winning combination!

Dave
(outside coach/consultant)

MMI is a company on the move—growing intelligently by executing a carefully crafted strategy to ensure sustained bottom-line growth, and cultivating a healthy organization that supports the livelihood of teammates and their families. Exceptional leadership is required to achieve organizational success. … MMI's leadership has created a strong and healthy organization that attracts talented workers … Once on board, teammates recognize the importance and value placed on them by the company's leadership. That recognition instills individual dedication and pride, which further increases the strength and health of the organization.

Mark
(business colleague)

It's a small enough, close-knit company that you are a person, not a number. If you put forth the effort and show dedication, training and advancements are limitless. [I love] the fact that we can text a picture to the owner. LOL. It's not "just some factory job"; it's a place where you can build your career.

Kristen
(MMI employee)

It is so fun being part of an organization that is growing and where everyone works hard to accomplish the same goal. This is truly the nicest group of people to work with, and that is hard to find. :)

Jamee
(MMI employee)

"THE INDUSTRY"

It's also important to look at how we are objectively evaluated by industry outsiders who have no stake whatsoever in the company. We take great pride in the fact that we have achieved a number of awards from prestigious organizations. Although we don't work for the awards—we work for our customers and our people—it's nice when the awards keep rolling in.

A few recent achievements: the Most Valuable Entrepreneur Award from *Corp!* magazine, the 2018 Economic Impact Award from Grow Michigan, and the Strategically Focused Award from the state of Michigan. I've been nominated this year for Ernst & Young's Entrepreneur of the Year award, and *Inc.* magazine has named MMI one of the fastest-growing companies in America. And those are just some of our most recent accolades.

Even more telling than our awards, though, is the market value the industry places on our organization. At least once or twice a week, I am contacted by private equity firms interested in buying the company. Recently, Deloitte, the globally known accounting and consulting firm, got in touch with us because of our reputation. They invited us to participate in a major annual event in which several uniquely promising companies pitch themselves to a group of about 175 private equity firms interested in investing. It's like *Shark*

Tank, only on a huge scale. Deloitte also did an in-depth analysis of the company, in which they calculated the company's value at $64 million. Not bad for a $250,000 investment on my part.

FOLLOWING THE RECIPE

The reason MMI has had such phenomenal success in only seven years is simple. We followed the recipe—the one I've been sharing with you for the last eight chapters:

- We base our business on a clear and simple set of values and goals that everyone understands.

- We communicate up, down, and sideways in a highly collaborative culture.

- We make sure every single employee thoroughly understands his/her role and how it is contributing to the company's success.

- We tell our people all the time, in every way we can, that they are the company's most important asset.

- We clearly display data to communicate how each shift is performing, every hour of every day, relative to the company's goals. We keep a scoreboard.

- We build benchmarks into our metrics so that we are all striving on a daily basis to be the best in class of our industry.

- We constantly review things like labor efficiency, product margins, scrap, waste, overtime, on-time delivery, and product quality, using measurable metrics.

- We tie each employee's SMART goals to the overall annual plan for the company and to the company's goals.

What about you? Are you doing what you love? Are you in this thing with both feet?

- We review those SMART goals every quarter, rather than wait till December to discover that employees may not be reaching their goals.

- We empower our people to make decisions and to take educated risks.

- We keep our value proposition front and center, every day.

- We seek out customers who are important to us and to whom we are important in return. We don't waste time chasing customers who aren't good for us.

- We keep our focus tight, taking only those jobs where our expertise can shine and where we can make a good and fair profit margin for the work we do.

- We reward our people for contributing to the company's success.

- We use cross-functional goals to ensure collaboration across all departments.

- We continually invest in our people, offering training, education, development, and advancement. We strive to be the place everyone wants to work.

It isn't rocket science, but it *is* a rocket that can launch your business into the stratosphere.

WHAT IS SUCCESS FOR YOU?

Will you apply the recipe in your own business? Only you can answer that. The first question you'll need to answer is, "Do these ideas make sense?" After reading these eight chapters, do the concepts presented here pass the head test and gut test? Do they make logical sense? Do they feel intuitively true? If so, then the only questions that remain are, "Do you really want this?" and, "How badly?"

Let's circle back to a point I made at the beginning of the book—the importance of defining success for yourself. In my career I've seen many people in leadership positions who, perhaps unconsciously, hold their businesses back from being all they can be. They often do this because they're afraid of losing control if the business grows bigger, or they're afraid of having to shift out of their comfort zone. So they sabotage their own growth. They *talk* about success, but they don't really want it.

I've also seen two opposing types of leader—those who are interested in *being* good and those who are interested in *looking* good. The latter are surprisingly common. These people are motivated to cover their own rear ends and to appear to others as if they are smart, powerful, and in charge. Their egos are running the show. They are full of fear. These people eventually crash and burn because they're not truly aligned with what is best for the company.

Those who are truly motivated by *being* good, however, are a rarer breed. They are the ones who eventually pull ahead in the race.

It all comes down to passion. To genuinely desire to *be* good, you must be passionate about your business.

Are you doing what you passionately want to do? I know the answer to that question for myself. I told you about the upper-eight-figure valuation that's recently been placed on my business. I admit, sometimes it's tempting to think of selling—taking a huge payday, buying a yacht, and disappearing to some island in the Mediterranean to live a life of luxury. But the honest truth is: right now, there's nothing I'd rather be doing than running MMI. If I sold the company, I'd be bored out of my mind in three days, and looking for a new business to start or buy.

That's me. I'm doing what I'm passionate about. I honestly don't know whether or not I might want to start another business someday, or whether I'll just continue to build MMI—through new product lines, new verticals, new locations, etc. But one thing I do know for sure: hope is not a plan. Whatever path I choose for the future, I know I finally have a recipe, a plan, for *making it happen*. And that knowledge makes me excited beyond belief about the future.

What about you? Are you doing what you love? Are you in this thing with both feet? Do you want to *look* good or *be* good? Whether you're an established business owner, a salaried leader, a start-up entrepreneur, or someone climbing the rungs of management, are you ready to stop hoping and grab the steering wheel? Then you're holding the road map in your hand.

I'm tempted to say, "Good luck," but I won't. Because luck isn't something you'll need.

You have a plan instead.

OUR SERVICES

MMI Engineered Solutions, Inc., is a tier-one injection-molding and tooling company headquartered in Saline, Michigan. We also have operations in Monterrey, Mexico; Warren, Michigan; and Troy, Michigan. MMI-es serves the automotive, heavy-truck, and industrial-automation industries. Our company operates with a very simple mission: we deliver a quality product, on time, at a competitive price. We believe our most important asset is our people. You can learn more about MMI-es at **www.MMI-es.com.**

ABOUT THE AUTHOR

Doug Callahan was born and raised in a car-loving Detroit family. He started his first business—a landscaping service—when he was twelve and built it until he became a designer for General Motors. From there he took on his first engineering role with an injection-molding supplier for the auto industry. During his tenure at that firm, he helped grow the business from around $20 million in sales to $300 million and learned the foundations of the business recipe he shares in this book.

In 2012, Doug took over operations of MMI Engineered Solutions, Inc. Using his unique management recipe, he has turned MMI into one of America's fastest-growing companies (*Inc.* magazine). Doug has a BSME and an MBA from Lawrence Technological University and a JD from the University of Detroit.